The
PEOPLE
ATLAS

Philip Steele

Oxford

Designed by Designers and Partners, Oxford
Illustrated by Adam and Christa Hook
(Linden Artists), John Downes and Steve Weston
Edited by Nicola Barber

Created and produced by
Ilex Publishers Limited
29-31 George Street
Oxford, England OX1 2AJ

Published in the United States of America by
Oxford University Press, Inc.,
200 Madison Avenue,
New York, N.Y. 10016

Oxford is a registered trademark of
Oxford University Press

Library of Congress
Cataloging-in-Publication Data
  Steele, Philip.
    The people atlas / Philip Steele.
      p.   cm.
    Includes index.
    Summary: Text and map spreads explore the peoples of the world and
  their culture, continent by continent.
    ISBN 0-19-520846-3
    1. Ethnology—Atlases—Juvenile literature.   2. Manners and
  customs—Atlases—Juvenile literature.   [1. Ethnology—Atlases.
  2. Manners and customs—Atlases.]   I. Title.
  GN333.S84   1991
  305.8—dc20   91-7242
                                                                      CIP
                                                                       AC

ISBN 0-19-520846-3

Printing (last digit): 9   8   7   6   5   4   3   2   1
Printed by Eurograph s.p.a. - Milano - Italy

CONTENTS

Introduction 6
Moving around the world 8

North America 10
Space Age Americans 12
Rawhide rodeo 13
Dragons of San Francisco 13
Life in an Inuit village 14
Did you know? 14
Words around the world 15

Latin America 16
Peoples of the Caribbean 18
Tropical seas and tourists 18
Sounds of the islands 18
Descendants of the Maya 19
The streets of Mexico City 19
People need trees 20
Weavers of the Andes 20
Riders of the *pampas* 21
Did you know? 21

Africa 22
Precious water 24
"In the name of Allah…" 24
The veiled ones 25
The cattle herders 25
The Nigerian capital 26
Sounds of Africa 26
Food around the world 27
Did you know? 28
Warriors of the Masai 29
The desert hunters 29

Europe 30
East meets West 32
Flamenco! 32
England v Wales 33
Europe united 34
Did you know? 34

Clothes around the world 35
A wealth of languages 36
Reindeer herders 37
On the move 37

Soviet Union 38
Blessed is our God… 40
Women at work 40
Did you know? 40
Houses around the world 41

Asia 42
Women of the desert 44
Holy wars 44
Money around the world 45
A life together 46
Life on top of the world 47
A Dani village 48
Silver and beads 48
Javanese puppetry 49
Did you know? 49

The Far East 50
Life as a Chinese student 52
The Tibetan way of life 52
Did you know? 52
The soybean story 53
Rice farming in Japan 53
Festival time 53

Oceania 54
The peopling of a continent 56
The Maori people 57
The gift of a pig 58
Shell money 58
Did you know? 59
Fire-walkers of Fiji 59

Glossary 60
Index 62

INTRODUCTION

NORTH AMERICA

ATLANTIC OCEAN

TEXAN COWBOY

CENTRAL AMERICA

PACIFIC OCEAN

A crowded planet
The most crowded place in the world is the territory of Hong Kong, on the southern coast of China. In parts of Hong Kong there are over 13,500 people living in an area of one square mile. Bangladesh is the most crowded of the larger countries, with over 1,800 people for every square mile. Greenland is the emptiest country, with only one person for every 16 square miles of land.

O F THE nine planets that circle the Sun, only on Earth is life possible. Air, light, water, and warmth have made our planet a home for a vast variety of plants and animals. However, human beings are recent arrivals in the history of life on Earth. The earliest living cells probably developed in Earth's oceans about four billion years ago; "modern" human beings (*Homo sapiens*) appeared only 40,000 years ago. They proved to be successful hunters, and, by 10,000 years ago, had also learned to grow crops and keep animals. At this time, only about six million people lived in the whole world.

Today, the population of the world is about 5,300 million. Humans live in deserts and jungles, and in cities. They travel around the planet by land, sea, or air. They have climbed the highest mountains and visited the depths of the oceans. They have even left their home planet and traveled in Space.

AMERICAN INDIANS, BOLIVIA

SOUTH AMERICA

Peoples of the Americas
The first American peoples were the Inuit (Eskimos) and American Indians. At the time of the European "discovery" of America in the fifteenth century, more than 600 different Indian cultures and societies existed in the American continent. These native peoples were gradually outnumbered by settlers from Europe, and by the black people they brought with them from West Africa. Many of today's Americans are of mixed descent.

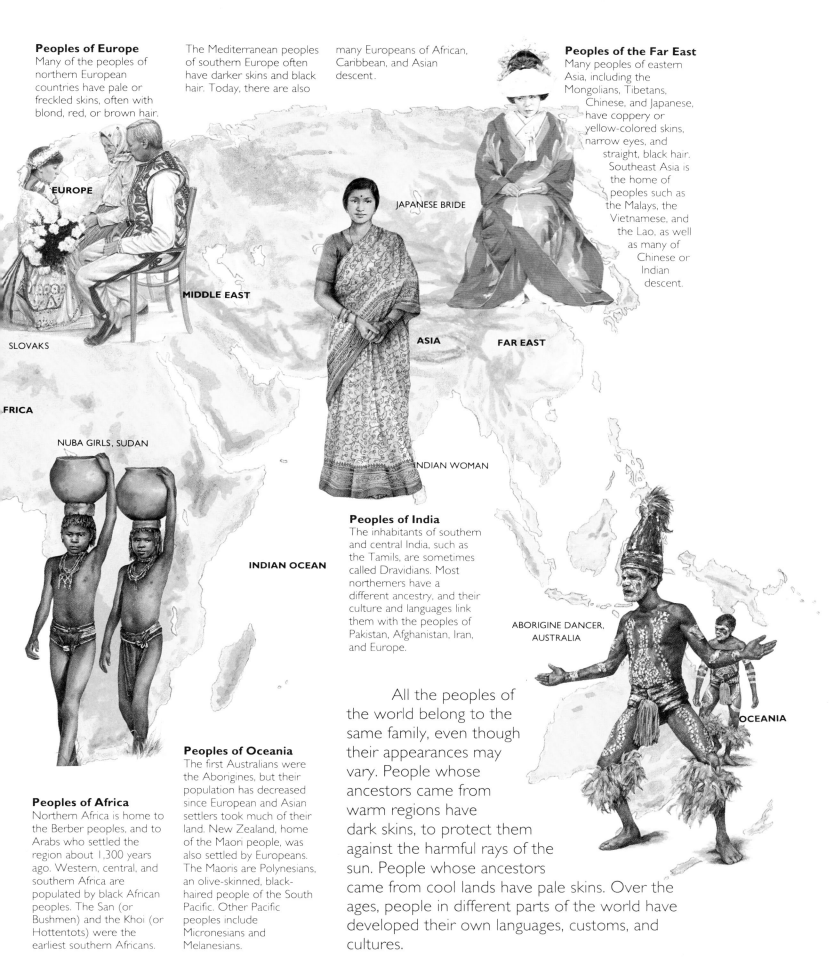

Peoples of Europe

Many of the peoples of northern European countries have pale or freckled skins, often with blond, red, or brown hair. The Mediterranean peoples of southern Europe often have darker skins and black hair. Today, there are also many Europeans of African, Caribbean, and Asian descent.

EUROPE

MIDDLE EAST

SLOVAKS

AFRICA

NUBA GIRLS, SUDAN

JAPANESE BRIDE

ASIA

FAR EAST

INDIAN WOMAN

Peoples of the Far East

Many peoples of eastern Asia, including the Mongolians, Tibetans, Chinese, and Japanese, have coppery or yellow-colored skins, narrow eyes, and straight, black hair. Southeast Asia is the home of peoples such as the Malays, the Vietnamese, and the Lao, as well as many of Chinese or Indian descent.

Peoples of India

The inhabitants of southern and central India, such as the Tamils, are sometimes called Dravidians. Most northerners have a different ancestry, and their culture and languages link them with the peoples of Pakistan, Afghanistan, Iran, and Europe.

INDIAN OCEAN

ABORIGINE DANCER, AUSTRALIA

OCEANIA

Peoples of Oceania

The first Australians were the Aborigines, but their population has decreased since European and Asian settlers took much of their land. New Zealand, home of the Maori people, was also settled by Europeans. The Maoris are Polynesians, an olive-skinned, black-haired people of the South Pacific. Other Pacific peoples include Micronesians and Melanesians.

Peoples of Africa

Northern Africa is home to the Berber peoples, and to Arabs who settled the region about 1,300 years ago. Western, central, and southern Africa are populated by black African peoples. The San (or Bushmen) and the Khoi (or Hottentots) were the earliest southern Africans.

All the peoples of the world belong to the same family, even though their appearances may vary. People whose ancestors came from warm regions have dark skins, to protect them against the harmful rays of the sun. People whose ancestors came from cool lands have pale skins. Over the ages, people in different parts of the world have developed their own languages, customs, and cultures.

MOVING AROUND THE WORLD

American Indians

The first peoples migrated to the American continent from Asia between twenty and forty thousand years ago, across a land bridge caused by the fall in sea levels during the last Ice Age. By 12,000 years ago, they had reached the southernmost tip of South America. From 1000 BC until the arrival of the Europeans, great civilizations flourished in both Central and South America.

In 1947, a Norwegian explorer called Thor Heyerdahl decided to test his theories about the movements of ancient peoples around the world. He sailed a balsa wood raft called the *Kon-Tiki* across the Pacific Ocean, in an attempt to prove that the Polynesian peoples may have originated in South America.

VIKINGS

JOHN AND SEBASTIAN CABOT 1497

AMERICAN INDIANS

CHRISTOPHER COLUMBUS 1492-3

AMERIGO VESPUCCI 1499-1501

THOR HEYERDAHL 1947

THE earliest members of the human tribe evolved in Africa, about four million years ago. Since then, humans have spread around the world. Early peoples wandered in search of food, gathering plants and hunting. Gradually, some people began to cultivate crops and domesticate certain animals. The first farmers settled on land around the Tigris, Euphrates, and Nile rivers, in an area that is often referred to as the "Fertile Crescent." They learned to make tools and work metal, and to trade with each other.

As different peoples came into contact with each other, languages and new ideas spread, but sometimes there was conflict. People invaded other lands and made slaves of the inhabitants, carrying them off to other countries. Sometimes different peoples were brought together under the rule of a powerful kingdom or empire. As a result, the borders of many countries today include peoples of different origins, who speak various languages.

The Bantu speakers

Today, many African peoples speak languages belonging to the Bantu group. Bantu languages probably originated around the Benue and Niger rivers in western Africa. The languages were passed on by peoples skilled in iron-working. Over thousands of years, many of these peoples migrated south. By the eighteenth century, Bantu culture and language had reached the southern coast of Africa.

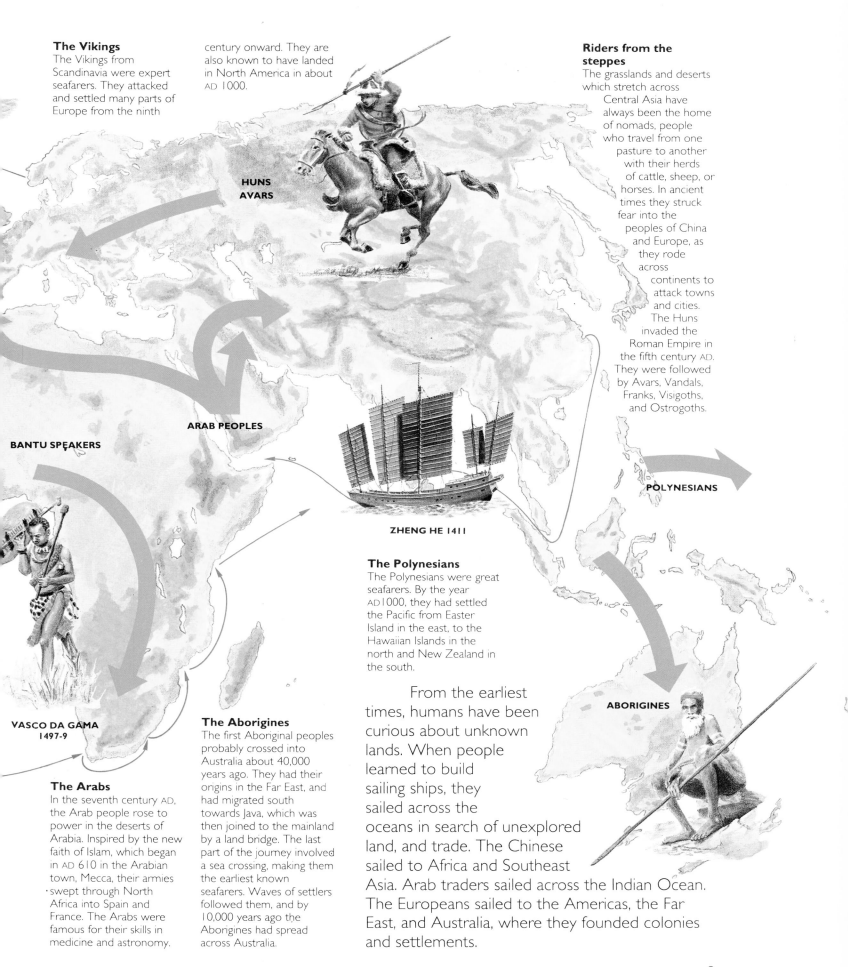

The Vikings
The Vikings from Scandinavia were expert seafarers. They attacked and settled many parts of Europe from the ninth century onward. They are also known to have landed in North America in about AD 1000.

HUNS AVARS

ARAB PEOPLES

BANTU SPEAKERS

Riders from the steppes
The grasslands and deserts which stretch across Central Asia have always been the home of nomads, people who travel from one pasture to another with their herds of cattle, sheep, or horses. In ancient times they struck fear into the peoples of China and Europe, as they rode across continents to attack towns and cities. The Huns invaded the Roman Empire in the fifth century AD. They were followed by Avars, Vandals, Franks, Visigoths, and Ostrogoths.

ZHENG HE 1411

POLYNESIANS

The Polynesians
The Polynesians were great seafarers. By the year AD 1000, they had settled the Pacific from Easter Island in the east, to the Hawaiian Islands in the north and New Zealand in the south.

VASCO DA GAMA 1497-9

ABORIGINES

The Arabs
In the seventh century AD, the Arab people rose to power in the deserts of Arabia. Inspired by the new faith of Islam, which began in AD 610 in the Arabian town, Mecca, their armies swept through North Africa into Spain and France. The Arabs were famous for their skills in medicine and astronomy.

The Aborigines
The first Aboriginal peoples probably crossed into Australia about 40,000 years ago. They had their origins in the Far East, and had migrated south towards Java, which was then joined to the mainland by a land bridge. The last part of the journey involved a sea crossing, making them the earliest known seafarers. Waves of settlers followed them, and by 10,000 years ago the Aborigines had spread across Australia.

From the earliest times, humans have been curious about unknown lands. When people learned to build sailing ships, they sailed across the oceans in search of unexplored land, and trade. The Chinese sailed to Africa and Southeast Asia. Arab traders sailed across the Indian Ocean. The Europeans sailed to the Americas, the Far East, and Australia, where they founded colonies and settlements.

NORTH AMERICA

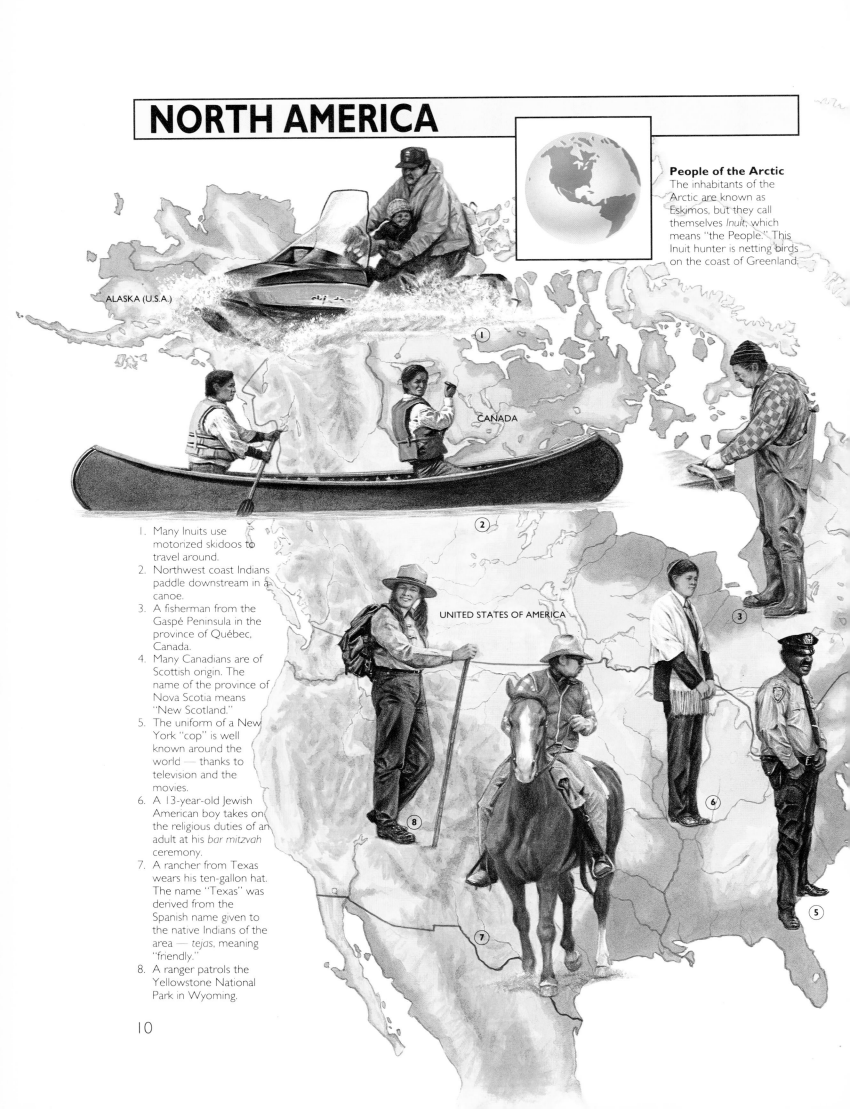

People of the Arctic
The inhabitants of the Arctic are known as Eskimos, but they call themselves *Inuit*, which means "the People." This Inuit hunter is netting birds on the coast of Greenland.

ALASKA (U.S.A.)

CANADA

UNITED STATES OF AMERICA

1. Many Inuits use motorized skidoos to travel around.
2. Northwest coast Indians paddle downstream in a canoe.
3. A fisherman from the Gaspé Peninsula in the province of Québec, Canada.
4. Many Canadians are of Scottish origin. The name of the province of Nova Scotia means "New Scotland."
5. The uniform of a New York "cop" is well known around the world — thanks to television and the movies.
6. A 13-year-old Jewish American boy takes on the religious duties of an adult at his *bar mitzvah* ceremony.
7. A rancher from Texas wears his ten-gallon hat. The name "Texas" was derived from the Spanish name given to the native Indians of the area — *tejas*, meaning "friendly."
8. A ranger patrols the Yellowstone National Park in Wyoming.

NORTH America is a vast continent. It stretches from the pack ice of the Arctic to the tropical waters of the Gulf of Mexico. Between the Pacific and the Atlantic coasts lie 2,900 miles (4,700 kilometers) of mountain, desert, forest, and prairie. The United States of America occupies the central part of this land mass, as well as Alaska, in the northwest. Canada extends across the snowy northern wastes toward Greenland.

The first Americans came from the Siberian region of Asia, which was once joined to America. These "American Indians" arrived between twenty and forty thousand years ago. About 1,000 years ago, Viking warriors sailed to North America from Europe. However, it was not until about 400 years ago that Europeans made permanent settlements in North America.

Razzmatazz
The big parade passes through Washington D.C., the American capital. Drum majorettes step along the streets, twirling their batons. Horsemen wear the cowboy dress of the old West. Presiding over the celebrations is the traditional American figure of "Uncle Sam."

11

Today, the United States of America forms one single nation with its own way of life. However, many of its peoples like to keep up the traditions of their ancestors. In different parts of the United States you may see colorful public festivals, or join in celebrations which have their origins in American Indian, African, Jewish, Armenian, or Hispanic traditions. Some towns have maintained links with the countries from which the settlers came, and bear names familiar in the "Old World," such as Paris, Harlem, Norfolk, and Naples.

On the fourth Thursday in November, Thanksgiving Day is celebrated throughout the United States. This is the day on which the Massachusetts Pilgrims first gave thanks for a year's survival in the "New World." These English settlers sailed to America on a ship called the *Mayflower*, in 1620.

INDIAN RESERVES

This gray granite temple in Salt Lake City, Utah, is the center of the Mormon faith. It took 40 years to complete after its foundations were laid in 1853. The Mormon faith was started in New England by Joseph Smith in 1827, and brought to Utah by Brigham Young. Mormons are taught to lead disciplined, healthy lives: they do not smoke, or drink coffee or alcohol.

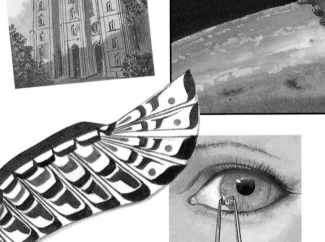

The first Americans

A giant carved totem pole guards an Indian village. On the northwest Pacific coast of the United States and Canada, Indian tribes once lived by fishing and whaling. In other regions they lived by farming, or by hunting the herds of bison which used to roam the prairies.

Many of these native Americans were killed in the wars against the white settlers during the last century. Others died from previously unknown diseases brought in by the Europeans.

About one and a half million native Americans live in the United States today, and a half million more live in Canada. Many still live on tribal lands, but they have had to adapt

The modern world relies on computers. Between 1958 and 1969, American scientists invented ways of making computers very small. The working instructions were placed on a tiny slice of crystal of a substance called silicon. This "microchip" is smaller than the iris of a human eye. So many computer firms are now based in California that part of the state is known as "Silicon Valley."

their old ways of life. One of the largest Indian nations in the United States is that of the Navajo, most of whom live on a reservation in the southwest.

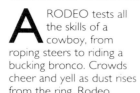

and the U.S. have important space exploration projects. The Russians were the first to put a man into space, but the first people to land on the Moon were Americans. Since then space probes have photographed Mars, Neptune, Venus, Saturn, and Uranus.

Rawhide rodeo

A RODEO tests all the skills of a cowboy, from roping steers to riding a bucking bronco. Crowds cheer and yell as dust rises from the ring. Rodeo competitions are popular from Texas to Canada, and help to keep alive the old traditions of the Wild West.

The great days of the cowboys were in the last century, when they drove huge herds of cattle across country to railroad towns. From there, trains took the cattle to the stockyards of Chicago. Many poor European immigrants, black people, and Indians became cowboys. Films have shown the cowboy's life as exciting. In reality it was mostly dull, dirty, back-breaking work.

Harlem, New York

Playing basketball in Harlem, New York. The population of this suburb is almost entirely made up of black people, and people of Hispanic origin. The rows of brownstones which line the Harlem streets were

built at the turn of the century. The first black people began to move into Harlem in the 1900's, and by the 1920's it had become established as a "ghetto" — an area of a city in which people of one race all live together.

Dragons of San Francisco

CHINESE-American dancers weave through the streets of San Francisco as part of their New Year celebrations. They carry a beautiful paper dragon to bring good luck. San Francisco has the largest Chinese community outside Asia.

Chinese people first came to live in the United States in the nineteenth century, as they fled from war and famine in their own country. At first they were unwelcome immigrants, but this attitude changed when cheap labor was needed to build railroads across the country. Today, there are over 800,000 Chinese-Americans.

Religious communities

Many Europeans fled to the "New World" because they were not allowed to follow their own faiths in their home countries. The Mennonites were a religious group, or sect, founded in Switzerland in 1523. In 1620 a new sect, the Amish, broke away from them in turn. Both Amish and Mennonites arrived in North America about 1720. They set up farming villages in the United States and Canada. Many still wear plain, home-made clothes and no jewelry, and some still refuse to use telephones or electric power. Many drive horses and carts rather than automobiles.

In area, Canada is the second largest country in the world: it covers 3,850,000 square miles (nearly ten million square kilometers). However, only 25 million people live in Canada — less than a tenth of the population of the United States. Much of the vast northern territories is covered by forest or ice. The big cities are all in the milder south, near the border with the United States. Canadians make their living from growing wheat, mining, fishing, industry, and business.

Life in an Inuit village

THE homeland of the Inuit, or Eskimos, is called *Inuit Nunangat* or "Land of the People." It stretches for more than 4,000 miles (6,500 kilometers), and includes the Arctic coasts of Greenland, Canada, Alaska, and a small part of the Soviet Union.

The Arctic has changed rapidly in recent years. Oil and mining companies have moved in and, where there were once only huts of stone and turf, now small towns of wooden houses have been built with stores and schools. Dog sledges have been replaced by motor-driven "skidoos" and for long journeys, light aircraft or helicopters are used.

The older Inuit remember a way of life in which nothing was wasted. Seals or caribou provided food, clothing, fat, oil, skins, and bone. Today's way of life often seems wasteful and purposeless to them, and they fear that the younger Inuit will never know the traditional way of life, but want to live like the white people who have taken over their land.

Timber!

Many Canadian workers must battle with the elements in order to make a living. The fishermen of Newfoundland risk their lives in foggy and stormy seas. The lumberjacks of the Canadian forests live in remote logging camps in the snowy countryside.

However, modern transport and better communications have, to some extent, tamed the wilderness. Canada has more than two million square miles (four million square kilometers) of forest, and over half of this is used for lumber. Giant evergreens are cut down with saws and either loaded onto huge trucks, or floated down rivers to the mills. The timber is sawed into planks and used for building or furniture. Some is pulped and made into paper.

DID YOU KNOW?

If you live in the United States you may live and work in the clouds. The Sears Tower in Chicago is 1,453 feet (443 meters) high and has 110 stories. The top 50 stories of the John Hancock Center, also in Chicago, is home to 1,500 residents. They need never step outside their home in the skies: the skyscraper has banks, restaurants, shops, a fitness center and swimming pool, offices, and a parking lot.

Forty percent of Canadians can trace their ancestry back to Great Britain, 27 percent to France and about 25 percent to other European countries. Inuit and Indians make up only one and a half percent of the total Canadian population.

IZWI *Shona* • ΛΕΞΙΣ *Greek* • ITZ *Basque* • SZÓ *Magyar* • คำ *Thai* • KATA *Malay and Indonesian*

MOT *French* • KELIME *Turkish* • 言葉 *Japanese* • ORD *Swedish* • GAIR *Welsh* • RIJEC *Serbo-Croat*

WORDS AROUND THE WORLD

AROUND the edge of this page are all kinds of words. Each means "word" in a different language. About 5,000 languages are spoken in the world today.

The first words were probably grunts and simple noises. Slowly, early humans began to give meanings to these sounds. People of the same tribe used the same words, and when they traded with people of other tribes, or moved to new lands, they learned new words and began to use them as well.

The first people known to write words were the Sumerians, in about 3200 BC. They used wedge shaped marks, pressed in clay, probably to keep a record of their goods for trading. The ancient Egyptians developed their own picture writing, called hieroglyphs. They also invented a new, and more convenient, material on which to write – papyrus, made from the papyrus reed. From this comes our modern word, paper.

Today, over 65 different alphabets are in use around the world, including the Roman alphabet used by English language speakers, and the Cyrillic script used by Russian, Serbian, and Bulgarian speakers. The language spoken by the most people in the world is Standard, or Mandarin, Chinese. It is written in over 50,000 different symbols, called "characters." Many of today's languages are related to each other; for example, most European and many Asian tongues belong to the same family known as the Indo-European group of languages.

①

②

1. A Sumerian clay tablet from about 3000 BC. It is probably a list of names, with the deep cuts representing numbers.
2. Egyptian picture writing, or hieroglyphs. This inscription was made in about 2100 BC.

Languages today
The diagram shows, in percentages, the number of people who speak the most widespread languages in the world.

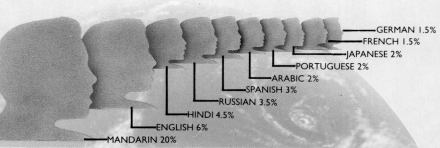

GERMAN 1.5%
FRENCH 1.5%
JAPANESE 2%
PORTUGUESE 2%
ARABIC 2%
SPANISH 3%
RUSSIAN 3.5%
HINDI 4.5%
ENGLISH 6%
MANDARIN 20%

LATIN AMERICA

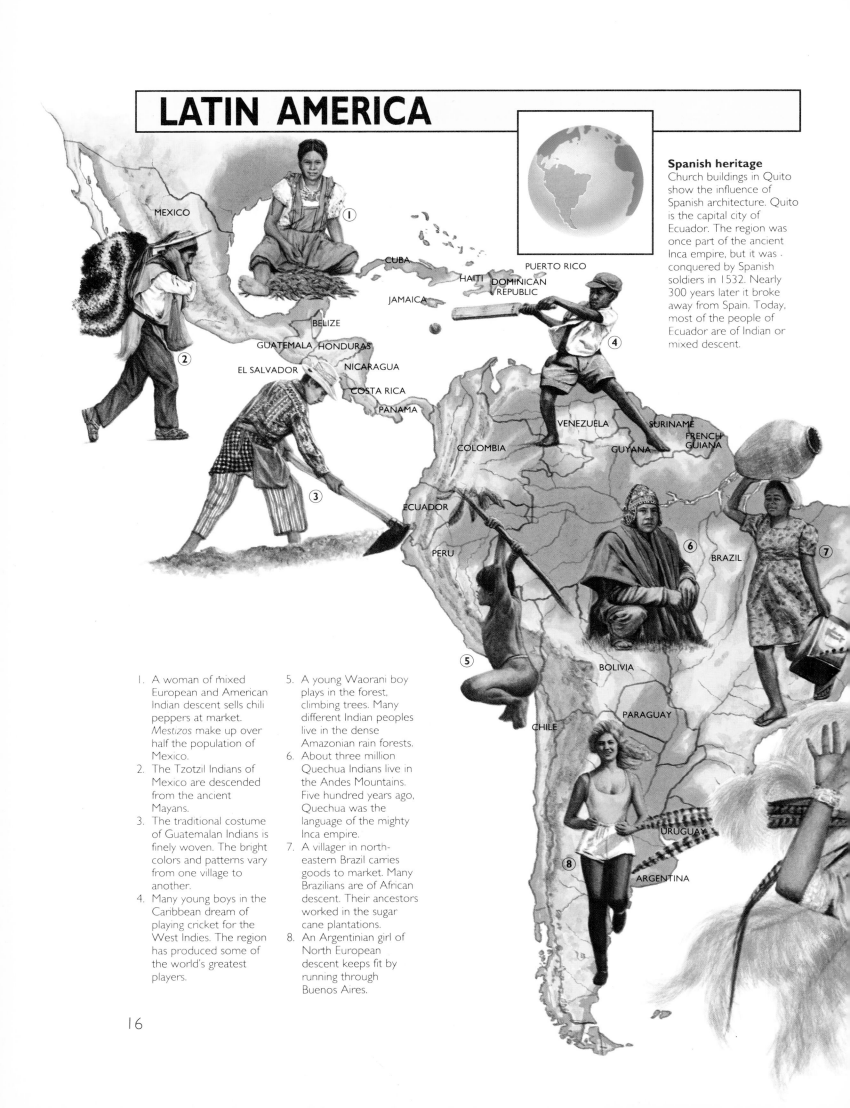

Spanish heritage
Church buildings in Quito show the influence of Spanish architecture. Quito is the capital city of Ecuador. The region was once part of the ancient Inca empire, but it was conquered by Spanish soldiers in 1532. Nearly 300 years later it broke away from Spain. Today, most of the people of Ecuador are of Indian or mixed descent.

MEXICO

CUBA

PUERTO RICO

HAITI DOMINICAN REPUBLIC

JAMAICA

BELIZE

GUATEMALA HONDURAS

EL SALVADOR NICARAGUA

COSTA RICA

PANAMA

VENEZUELA SURINAME FRENCH GUIANA

COLOMBIA GUYANA

ECUADOR

PERU

BRAZIL

BOLIVIA

PARAGUAY

CHILE

URUGUAY

ARGENTINA

1. A woman of mixed European and American Indian descent sells chili peppers at market. *Mestizos* make up over half the population of Mexico.

2. The Tzotzil Indians of Mexico are descended from the ancient Mayans.

3. The traditional costume of Guatemalan Indians is finely woven. The bright colors and patterns vary from one village to another.

4. Many young boys in the Caribbean dream of playing cricket for the West Indies. The region has produced some of the world's greatest players.

5. A young Waorani boy plays in the forest, climbing trees. Many different Indian peoples live in the dense Amazonian rain forests.

6. About three million Quechua Indians live in the Andes Mountains. Five hundred years ago, Quechua was the language of the mighty Inca empire.

7. A villager in north-eastern Brazil carries goods to market. Many Brazilians are of African descent. Their ancestors worked in the sugar cane plantations.

8. An Argentinian girl of North European descent keeps fit by running through Buenos Aires.

16

TO THE south of the Rio Grande River, the North American continent narrows, forming a land bridge between North and South America. Mexico, with its landscape of volcanoes, deserts, and forests, curves southward to the Yucatán peninsula. The smaller Central American countries lie to its south, on the narrow strip of land between the Pacific Ocean and the Caribbean Sea. The tropical islands of the Caribbean stretch east toward the Atlantic.

The long chain of the Andes Mountains forms a wall down the western side of South America. In the basin of the great Amazon River lie vast, steamy rain forests. To the south are grassy plains and rocky plateaus, stretching toward the stormy waters of Cape Horn.

Samba through Rio
When carnival was first held in Brazil, people threw flour and sand and perfumed water at each other. Today, Rio's spectacular carnival lasts for four days. The final parade includes up to 80,000 people, wearing glittering costumes and headdresses and dancing the *samba*. The best "samba school" is awarded the title, "Champion of the Avenue."

The lake in the sky
Lake Titicaca lies high in the Andes Mountains, between Bolivia and Peru. The shores of the lake are home to the Aymara Indians. In the harsh mountain climate they live on what they can cultivate in the arid soil, and by fishing in the lake from reed boats.

The first Europeans arrived in Central and South America in the sixteenth century. They conquered the powerful Indian empires they found there, and set up profitable plantations and gold mines. They transported slaves from Africa, and later poor laborers from Asia, to work on their land. Today, Central and South America is often referred to as "Latin America." This is because many of their peoples speak the languages of those European settlers, Portuguese and Spanish. Both of these languages stem from the ancient Latin tongue.

17

Saba's islanders

Saba is a tiny, mountainous island in the Leeward Islands. When it was discovered in 1493, by Christopher Columbus, it was home to Carib Indians, but in 1632 it was taken over by the Dutch. However, its white inhabitants are not all Dutch; some claim to be descended from British pirates who captured the island in 1655. Today, the island is still part of the Netherlands Antilles.

Peoples of the Caribbean

WHEN Christopher Columbus sailed to the Caribbean from Spain in 1492, he found the islands inhabited by American Indians - the Arawak, Tanala, and Carib tribes. But in the sixteenth and seventeenth centuries, Spanish, French, British, and Dutch people settled on the islands, and many of these Indians were killed. The new European settlers grew sugar and tobacco on the islands, and brought slaves from West Africa to work on their plantations. In the last 30 years, many Caribbean islands have become independent. Others, such as Martinique, which is part of France, are still ruled by European countries.

GUADELOUPE

DOMINICA

MARTINIQUE

ST. LUCIA

ST. VINCENT

GRENADA

Tropical seas and tourists

THE Caribbean is famous for its warm blue seas, fringed by white sands and palm trees. Underwater coral reefs are home to thousands of brightly colored fish.

Nearly one million tourists visit the island of Jamaica each year. Tourism brings much-needed money to many Caribbean islands, but sometimes threatens their natural world. Rare corals and turtle shells are taken for souvenirs, and some species are in danger of dying out.

Schoolgirls from the largest of the Caribbean islands, Cuba, at work in the fields. Many Cuban schoolchildren attend free boarding schools situated in the countryside. Their time is divided between studying at their desks and farm work. Of the many crops grown in Cuba, the most important are sugar cane and tobacco.

Sounds of the islands

THE mixture of peoples living on the islands of the Caribbean has given birth to all kinds of song and dance styles. Most have been strongly influenced by African rhythms. Calypso, soca, bluebeat, ska, and reggae all started life in the West Indies. Stars such as Bob Marley have made reggae music popular all over the world.

Many reggae songs are inspired by the Rastafarian faith. Rastafarians believe that the African land of Ethiopia is their spiritual home, but that they are in "Babylon," a state of exile.

Descendants of the Maya

IN THE Mexican state of Yucatán, Maya women chat as boiled kernels of corn are ground into flour. This flour will be mixed into dough and used to make *tortillas*, thin, rounded cakes of bread which are baked on a griddle and served with beans.

The Maya civilization was one of the great achievements of the American Indian culture. Between 300 BC and AD1519 the Maya built great cities and temples, and became skilled mathematicians and astronomers.

A young Mexican girl proudly enters the ring, showing off her riding skills in a *charreada*. This is a display and contest of skill in horse riding and lassoing that is found only in Mexico, although it is similar to the rodeos of North America (see *page 13*). The girl rides sidesaddle and wears traditional dress – including a broad-brimmed hat, or *sombrero*, to shield her head from the hot sun.

The streets of Mexico City

OLD tin tubs and buckets serve as baths and showers for these children in the slums of Mexico City. The Mexican capital is the largest city in the world. Over ten million people live in its center, and seven million more people live in its sprawling suburbs.

Today, the population of Mexico's towns and cities continues to grow, swollen by country people, known as *campesinos*, who come in search of work.

Many of these people are very poor. They live in slums and shanty towns. In Mexico City, a group of about one thousand people lives in caves cut into a steep hillside. The Mexican capital lies in an earthquake zone and the tremors that occasionally rock the city can cause great damage and destruction, adding to the difficulty of peoples' lives.

From 1200 BC, the region that is now called Mexico was the center of many ancient Indian civilizations, the last and most famous being that of the Aztecs. In 1519, a group of Spanish *conquistadores* (conquerors), led by Hernán Cortés, invaded and conquered the Aztec people. Today, most of the Mexican population is a mixture of Indian and Spanish blood, known as *mestizo*. Spanish is still spoken by 92 percent of the Mexican people, but over five million Mexicans talk dialects of Indian languages, such as Náhuatl, Maya, Zapotec, Otomi, and Mixtec.

To the southeast of Mexico lie the seven, smaller Central American countries. They, too, have mixed populations; for example, Guatemala is largely peopled by descendants of Maya and Quiché Indians, but most of the people of Costa Rica have a Spanish ancestry, with some black peoples and some Indians in the south.

Fighting for survival

A Kayapo chief wears the traditional broad lip plate of his tribe, stuck into his lower lip. The Kayapo Indians live in the Brazilian state of Pará, in the Amazonian rain forest. Many of them have died from diseases brought into the area by outsiders. Miners have tried to steal their land, which is rich in gold.

The Kayapo have fought for their lands and their rights with great skill. By campaigning with modern methods, they have managed to keep their lands and preserve their traditional ways of life.

Many people, including children, pull together a meager living in the shanty towns of South America. A refuse dump provides scraps of food, or old cans that can be sold. The centers of cities such as Rio de Janeiro are modern and wealthy, but around their edges lie the flimsy homes of the poor. Here, there are no proper drains or water supplies.

People need trees

THE rain forests around the Amazon River are the biggest in the world. They spread for thousands of miles to the north and south of the Equator. Trees, ferns, and creepers form a dense blanket of vegetation that is home to thousands of different species of plants and animals.

Many Indian peoples also live in the rain forest. It is thought that there are about 180 Amazonian Indian tribes, and their traditional ways of life complement their environment, rather than destroying it. They clear small spaces near their settlements where they can grow corn, sweet potatoes, and manioc (a bitter root vegetable). They hunt and fish. Every ten years or so they move on to a new part of the forest.

NORTHERN PERIMETER HIGHWAY   BELÉM

PAN-AMERICAN HIGHWAY

TRANS-AMAZONIAN HIGHWAY

BELÉM-BRASÍLIA HIGHWAY

BRASÍLIA

AREA OF AMAZONIAN RAIN FOREST

Weavers of the Andes

Best clothes are worn for market, high in the Bolivian Andes. The people who inhabit these highland areas are mostly of Indian descent. They live by herding llamas, alpacas, and vicuñas. Hair and wool are taken from these animals, as well as from sheep, and spun into yarn. From this the women weave their brightly colored skirts, colorful striped blankets, shawls, and ponchos.

In the fifteenth century, many South American Indians lived under the rule of the Incas, an Indian tribe which originated in the southern Andes. At its largest extent, their empire covered modern Peru, Ecuador, Bolivia, northern Argentina, and northern Chile.

Since the Spanish conquest in the sixteenth century, the South American countries have been settled by people from all over the world. In French Guiana, for example, there are Haitians, French, and Chinese. In Suriname, people speak Dutch, English, Hindi, Chinese, and Javanese. Brazil is Portuguese speaking, but in all the other countries of South America, Spanish is the official language. In some areas, the languages of the American Indians are still spoken.

In recent years, many new people have moved into the forest. Road builders, engineers, prospectors, loggers, ranchers, and farmers have all left their mark on the rain forest. If the destruction of the forest is not stopped, there could be nothing left within 30 or 40 years. This would be a catastrophe for the Indians, and for people all over the world.

Riders of the *pampas*

To the south of the rain forests, and to the east of the Andes Mountains, lie grassy plains, known as *pampas*. This is cattle country, in which a ranch is called an *estancia*.

This *gaúcho*, or cowboy, wears traditional dress. His baggy trousers are tucked into high leather boots with spurs. He wears a neck scarf and a hat with a broad brim. Today, there are fewer large herds of cattle in Argentina, and the age of the *gaúcho* is disappearing fast. However, many Argentinians still admire the old way of life, and have not forgotten the riding skills perfected by the *gaúchos*.

Across the Atlantic

In 1865, a ship sailed to a remote part of southern Argentina called Patagonia, carrying 165 men, women, and children from Wales. This picture shows some of these brave immigrants. They wanted freedom to worship in their own way, and to speak their own language. Their descendants still live in Patagonia. Some continue to speak Welsh and keep in touch with the old country.

DID YOU KNOW?

LA PAZ

PUERTO WILLIAMS

South American Indians were the first to discover that the bark of the quinine tree contained a useful medicine. Many plants now common around the world were first grown in South America. These include the rubber tree, the pineapple, the cassava, the peanut, the green bean, and the vanilla pod.

The world's highest center of government is the Bolivian city of La Paz, which is 11,900 feet (3,630 meters) above sea level.

In 1532 the Spanish, under Francisco Pizarro, captured the Inca ruler Atahualpa by treachery. They forced the Incas to pay them a ransom worth more than $5,000,000. A whole hall was filled with gold and silver, but Atahualpa was killed.

The most southerly village in the world is Puerto Williams, on Isla Navarino in southern Chile.

The riddle of the desert

Fly in an aircraft over the deserts of southern Peru, and you will see a series of strange patterns on the ground below. Some look like spiders, some like monkeys or huge birds. Others are geometrical shapes. For many years, these shapes have puzzled archaeologists.

The patterns were made by Indians from the Nazca region, where a civilization grew up about 2,200 years ago. The lines were made by scraping away surface soil to reveal the bare rock beneath. The mysterious patterns may have been used as calendars.

21

AFRICA

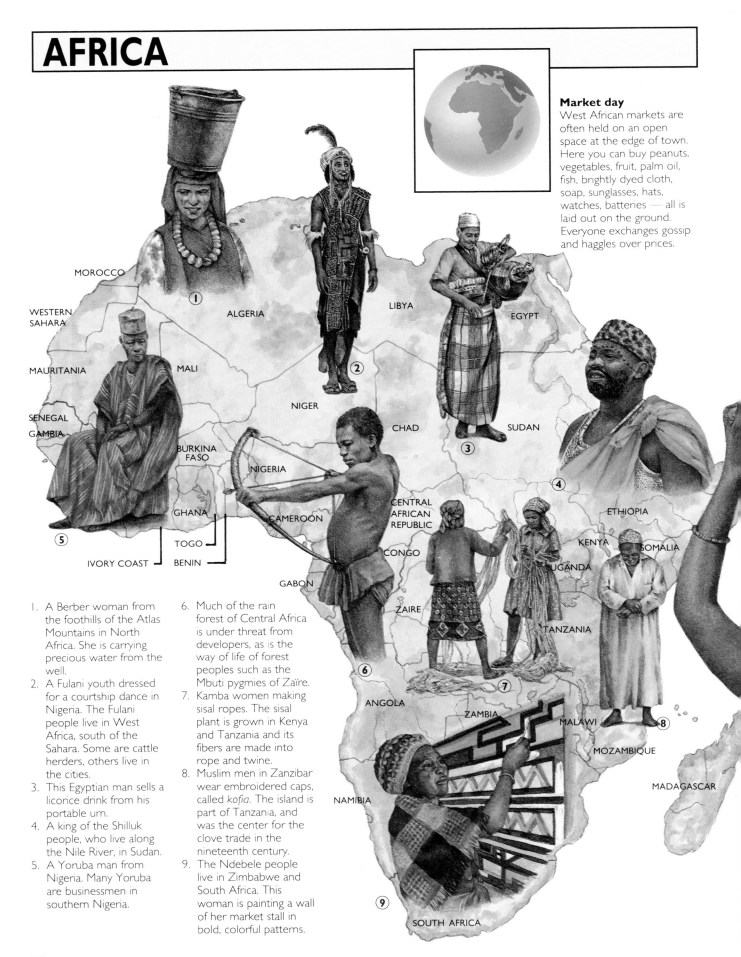

Market day
West African markets are often held on an open space at the edge of town. Here you can buy peanuts, vegetables, fruit, palm oil, fish, brightly dyed cloth, soap, sunglasses, hats, watches, batteries — all is laid out on the ground. Everyone exchanges gossip and haggles over prices.

MOROCCO

WESTERN SAHARA

MAURITANIA

SENEGAL

GAMBIA

ALGERIA

MALI

LIBYA

EGYPT

NIGER

CHAD

SUDAN

BURKINA FASO

NIGERIA

GHANA

CAMEROON

CENTRAL AFRICAN REPUBLIC

ETHIOPIA

KENYA

SOMALIA

UGANDA

CONGO

TOGO

IVORY COAST   BENIN

GABON

ZAIRE

TANZANIA

ANGOLA

ZAMBIA

MALAWI

MOZAMBIQUE

NAMIBIA

MADAGASCAR

SOUTH AFRICA

1. A Berber woman from the foothills of the Atlas Mountains in North Africa. She is carrying precious water from the well.
2. A Fulani youth dressed for a courtship dance in Nigeria. The Fulani people live in West Africa, south of the Sahara. Some are cattle herders, others live in the cities.
3. This Egyptian man sells a licorice drink from his portable urn.
4. A king of the Shilluk people, who live along the Nile River, in Sudan.
5. A Yoruba man from Nigeria. Many Yoruba are businessmen in southern Nigeria.

6. Much of the rain forest of Central Africa is under threat from developers, as is the way of life of forest peoples such as the Mbuti pygmies of Zaïre.
7. Kamba women making sisal ropes. The sisal plant is grown in Kenya and Tanzania and its fibers are made into rope and twine.
8. Muslim men in Zanzibar wear embroidered caps, called *kofia*. The island is part of Tanzania, and was the center for the clove trade in the nineteenth century.
9. The Ndebele people live in Zimbabwe and South Africa. This woman is painting a wall of her market stall in bold, colorful patterns.

Famine in the Sahel

About 50 million people live on the southern edge of the Sahara, in a region called the Sahel. Here there are frequent droughts, a period when no rain falls, causing the harvests to fail and herds of cattle to die. Famine follows. In 1983 about 300,000 people died of starvation in northern Ethiopia alone, and many more went hungry for months on end.

AFRICA is often called the "cradle of humankind" because the human race first began to develop there about four million years ago. The great civilization of the ancient Egyptians grew up along the fertile banks of the Nile River about 5,000 years ago. Farther south, kingdoms and empires flourished, hidden from the outside world by dense forests or burning deserts. The Nok civilization of Nigeria existed 2,000 years ago. Its people knew how to smelt iron and were fine sculptors. In southeastern Africa, the settlement of Great Zimbabwe was occupied from the fourth century AD. It grew to be a wealthy center for the gold trade. Its stone walls still stand today.

The useful calabash

A woman walks into market in Niger, with her baby slung on her back. A *calabash* is balanced on her head. These large gourds (dried vegetable shells) are used as storage containers and bowls. New calabashes may be bought in town and filled with provisions for the journey home. Cracked calabashes are easily repaired by sewing up the cracks with plant fiber.

European and Arab traders came to Africa in search of slaves, land, or wealth. In the last century, almost the whole continent was divided up into colonies. Only in the last 40 years has freedom returned to most of Africa. The same period has seen wars, famine, and hardship for many African peoples. Much of the continent is still wild and beautiful, the home of the world's last great herds of wild animals. However, there are also many large, modern towns, mines, and factories. People move to the cities in search of work, and forget the customs of their home villages. In the bush, many of those who once lived by hunting and gathering their food now work on farms.

Africa's northern coast borders the Mediterranean Sea. Along the coast the soil is fertile, but farther south, the landscape becomes harsher. Beyond the Atlas Mountains lie the seemingly endless, baking stretches of the Sahara.

Many peoples of the Sahara are nomads. For example, the Tuareg do not live in settled villages but move across the desert on their camels, traveling from one pasture to another with the seasons.

In northeastern Africa the Nile River winds through baking sand and rock, fringed by a narrow fertile strip. The Nile has two main tributaries. The White Nile flows through the largest area of swamp in the world, the Sudd — home to the Dinka and Nuer tribes; the Blue Nile rises in the highlands of Ethiopia. The two meet in Khartoum, the capital of Sudan.

Precious water

A SHADUF is a bucket on a long pole, used to raise water from the Nile River and pass it into channels to water the crops. This method of irrigation was developed by the Ancient Egyptians, 3,000 years ago, and is still used by many of the poorer Egyptian farmers today. Others have more modern methods of irrigation, using motor-driven wheels and pumps. Without the Nile, Egypt would not exist. For thousands of years, the river's

"In the name of Allah, the compassionate, the merciful ..."

A SCRIBE copies from the holy book of Islam, the Koran. In the year AD643 the Egyptian city of Alexandria was captured by Arabs. They brought with them a new faith: Islam. The religion spread along the north African coast, and nomads crossing the Sahara took the word of Muhammad south as far as Nigeria. Arab sailors founded mosques along Africa's east coast. Today, there are millions of Muslims in Africa, mainly in northern and central areas.

People of the Cross

The Christian religion has ancient roots in Africa. The Coptic church in Egypt is said to have been founded by St. Mark in the first century AD. Today, there are about three million Copts in Egypt.

About 40 percent of Ethiopians are Christians. The Ethiopian Orthodox Church was supported for hundreds of years by the emperor of the country. There are ancient churches cut into the rock of the mountains, and pilgrims walk long distances to visit holy shrines.

annual floods provided a lifeline to farmers in the Nile valley. The green of the fields still forms only a narrow strip along the banks. However, today the flood waters are controlled by a series of dams. To build the biggest of these, the Aswan Dam, a vast area of land was flooded, covering much of the grazing land of the Nubian peoples. Now life is easier for the Egyptian farmers, and their land produces two or three crops a year, instead of one.

Across the wilderness

Many roads in Africa, especially across the desert, are unmarked. Trucks and jeeps must lurch along dried river beds and avoid soft sand dunes. Travel across the world's largest desert, the Sahara, is particularly dangerous. In this land of rock, gravel, and sand, drivers must keep to the known routes, and check in at posts along the route. Spare fuel and water must be carried.

In ancient times, North Africa was the site of many great civilizations. The Egyptians farmed the valley of the Nile River, and built great temples and cities there. The Phoenicians and the Romans founded colonies along the Mediterranean coast. In the seventh century AD, the Arabs invaded and settled the region. In the last century, North Africa was colonized by the French, Spanish, and Italians, but today, the Arab nations of North Africa have achieved independence.

The veiled ones

THE word *tuareg* means "people of the veil." The Tuareg men wind long blue or black veils around their heads to protect themselves against the searing desert sun.

The Tuareg are experts in desert survival. Traditionally, they have lived in the western and southern Sahara, but in recent years, drought and famine have driven them south into Nigeria. For hundreds of years, the Tuareg controlled Saharan trade, transporting salt, gold, and ivory across the vast desert.

The cattle herders

SUDAN is Africa's largest country. In the north, the people are mainly Arab, but farther upstream, the round, thatched huts of the villages along the Nile are home to the people of the Dinka, Nuer, and Shilluk tribes. These people are cattle herders. They drink their cows' milk for food, and burn cattle dung to protect themselves from mosquitoes. In the vast area of swamp called the Sudd, Nuer and Dinka fishermen hunt from dugout canoes for their daily meals.

In the Nuba Mountains live the people of the Nuba tribe. These girls (*on the left*) are carrying water back to their hillside home, a daily chore that is essential for survival during the dry season.

The Nigerian capital

LAGOS is a busy, lively city. It is a great port and a center of industry and communications. It is also the fastest-growing city in Africa. Country people pour into the city in search of fame and fortune, but they rarely find either.

Housing is very poor. Three quarters of all families in Lagos must share one-room accommodation, and over 85 percent do not have a main water supply.

Yoruba women
Among the Yoruba people in Nigeria, the women run the markets while the men stay at home and cultivate the fields. Women still have to look after their families, cook, and fetch water from wells, often many miles from their homes, as well as helping their husbands at harvest time.

Villages in many parts of Nigeria and Mali have small round outbuildings made of dried mud. They are used to store grain, and are often raised off the ground. This keeps the grain dry, and beyond the reach of mice or rats. Millet and sorghum are the crops most widely grown in the dry areas. Rice is grown in the lusher, more humid regions.

Sounds of Africa

THE traditional music of Africa is based on drumming. African rhythms have influenced many of the musical styles of North and South America, especially jazz and blues.

Today, pop music is played from Mali to Zimbabwe. Many African bands have become well known in Europe and America. They often use electric guitars, drums, large brass sections, and backup singers. Many play in the "Dhluo" style, which originated in Kenya.

Zaïre stars such as Franco Luambo Makaidi and Mbilia Bel have become famous in Europe. The words of their songs may be in French, or in Lingalla, a language widely spoken around Kinshasa and along the river Zaïre.

To the south of the Sahara lies a dry, dusty belt of land called the Sahel. This region is home to the Fulani who graze their cattle there, and to the Hausa who cultivate the land. In the 1970's drought afflicted the Sahel, and now the cattle graze what survives of the thin grass, and the farmers fight an endless battle against the shifting desert sands. Many of the people have been forced to move away, often to a life of poverty in the cities.

Farther south the climate becomes more humid, there is more rain, and the soil is richer. Yams, cassava, and plantains are grown on small family plots and sold by the roadside. Large, modern cities such as Lagos are thronged with cars, buses, and trucks. To the east of the Gulf of Guinea lie the countries of Central Africa. Here are found rain forests that are home to Pygmy peoples, such as the Mbuti tribe.

FOOD AROUND THE WORLD

ALL the peoples of the world need a healthy, balanced diet. However, in some countries there is not enough food to go around, and many people are therefore malnourished. In the richer countries of the world, food is often wasted. As the number of hungry mouths increases, humans must learn to make better use of the land they farm, and the food they purchase.

"Staple" crops are those which form the basis of any diet. Wheat is a staple for many people, because it is used to make flour for bread. Rice is a staple in Asia, where it is eaten with almost every meal. Root crops, such as potatoes or cassava, also provide a staple food in many countries.

A great variety of fruit, vegetables, meat, and fish are prepared and eaten in different ways around the world. Hot spices, originally used to preserve food in hot climates, are popular in many countries. Tastes vary from one land to another. Most Westerners would hesitate before eating snake, rat, or insect grubs. However, many Asians eat no cheese, complaining that it is little more than rotting, soured milk.

1. The hamburger is made of ground beef and served on a bun. An American invention, this meal is now popular in many countries.
2. Mexican *tacos* are made from cornmeal, shaped into a thin pancake. Beans are seasoned with hot chili peppers. seasoned with hot chili peppers.
3. On the Ghana coast, cornmeal is steamed and kneaded into a dough called *kenkey*. It is eaten with fish.
4. French *cuisine*, or cooking, is famous around the world. Here a fresh seafood platter includes many kinds of shellfish found around the coast of Brittany.
5. An Indian meal is served with rice or a flat bread pancake called *chapati*. There are dishes of lentils, or *dal*, and a hot, spicy vegetable curry.
6. This meal comes from the Szechwan region of China. Rice is served with a dish of chopped pork and peanuts in a hot sauce. There are fresh greens as well.
7. Rice, seaweed, fish, beancurd, and vegetables form an important part of the diet in Japan. *Sushi* bars serve delicious raw fish and rice dishes.

A deep crack in the Earth runs through East Africa. It is called the Great Rift Valley, and is marked by a chain of long lakes between Uganda and Malawi as well as extinct volcanoes such as Kilimanjaro and Mount Kenya. At its far northern end live the Afar people, herders who survive in the arid desert lands around the Awash River. Farther south, in Kenya, Tanzania, and Uganda, huge herds of elephant, giraffe, and many other animals still roam the vast savanna lands. These were once also the hunting grounds of many African peoples, including the Masai. Today, many of these peoples have left their traditional homelands and settled in large cities, such as Nairobi and Mombasa.

DID YOU KNOW?

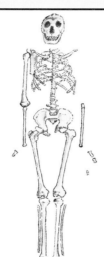

Fossils of some of the earliest human ancestors have been found in Africa. In 1985, a fossil skeleton was discovered near Lake Turkana, in Kenya. It had belonged to a boy and was 1,600,000 years old. It was of the type known as *Homo erectus* ("upright person").

The shortest people in the world are the Mbuti of Zaïre. Some Mbuti adult women are as small as 4 feet (1.24 meters).

The tallest people in the world are the Dinka of Sudan and the Tutsi of Rwanda and Burundi. Adult males of both peoples average a height of over 6 feet 5 inches (1.95 meters).

The earliest known stone tools were found in Ethiopia. They date back 2,500,000 years.

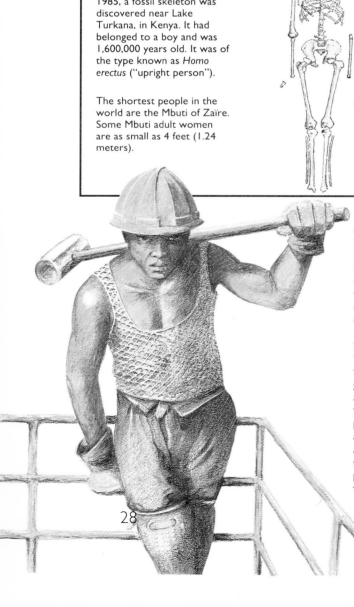

A land divided
In the past, the Xhosa lived by growing corn and keeping cattle. Today, many of them are migrant workers in the gold mines of South Africa, hundreds of miles from their homes.

Many black people in South Africa live in "homelands" created by the South African government. Black people are not allowed to vote for the government. Under the policy of *apartheid*, white and black peoples in South Africa live and work separately. There are now plans to bring this system to an end.

Warriors of the Masai

THE Masai people originally lived near the river Nile. About 400 years ago, they moved southward, driving their herds of cattle and goats before them, to settle on the plains around Kilimanjaro. The boundaries drawn by the Europeans in the last century divided their territory between two countries, now the independent states of Tanzania and Kenya. Much of the Masai's land was allocated to the European settlers, or, more recently, turned into game parks for the protection of African wildlife.

Despite the loss of their land, the Masai have fiercely protected their traditional ways of life. Their principal food is milk, although this is supplemented with blood taken from their cattle. Only rarely do they kill their cattle. They are too precious to eat all at once. Masai men are divided into age groups. At the age of 16 a youth becomes a *moran*, or warrior. He goes off to live in a separate camp called a *manyatta*. Here the Masai warriors carry long spears, braid their hair, and paint their bodies with ochre. They wear plugs and rings in their ears, and wrap themselves in distinctive scarlet cloaks.

Masai men may have several wives: a man's wealth may be measured by the number of wives he has! The women shave their heads and wear beaded headbands. Like the men, they wear necklaces and earrings. They live in their own separate huts.

The Zulus

Washing day comes round for a Zulu woman living in South Africa. There are over five and a half million people belonging to the Zulu tribe. Many live in the countryside. Others live in big cities such as Durban.

The Zulu nation rose to power about 200 years ago. It conquered neighboring peoples and fought bitter wars against the British under its great chief, Cetewayo.

	ARABIC, BERBER, AMHARIC		SAHARAN LANGUAGES
	WEST AFRICAN LANGUAGES		LANGUAGES OF THE NILE

NIGER-CONGO

BANTU

KHOISAN

AFRIKAANS, ENGLISH

MALAGASY

The spoken word

All kinds of languages and dialects are spoken in Africa. They reflect the great cultural wealth of the continent. In the north, many different dialects of Arabic and Berber are spoken. Amharic is the main tongue in Ethiopia.

Languages which grew up around the Nile River include Dinka, Nuer, Shilluk, and Luo. West African languages include Fufulde, Olof, and Akan.

South of the Equator, most African peoples speak languages belonging to the Bantu family. One of the most widespread of these is Swahili. Others include Shona, Xhosa, Zulu, and Ndebele.

The desert hunters

THE San people, or "Bushmen," once roamed all over southern Africa. Today their lands are confined to areas on the edge of the Kalahari Desert in Namibia, Botswana, Angola, and South Africa.

A small number of the San still live by hunting wild animals and gathering plants. They are experts at desert survival. They can find underground springs, and extract moisture from the roots of plants. Other San have settled on farms.

South of the Zambezi River, the map of Africa features two large deserts, the Kalahari and the Namib. South Africa itself is a country of mountains, grassy hills, and farmland where grapes and oranges can be grown.

In the last century, southern and eastern Africa were settled by the British, Dutch, Germans, and Portuguese. It was these Europeans who drew today's borders. Many of the African peoples have had a long fight to achieve freedom, and the struggle is not yet over in South Africa.

EUROPE

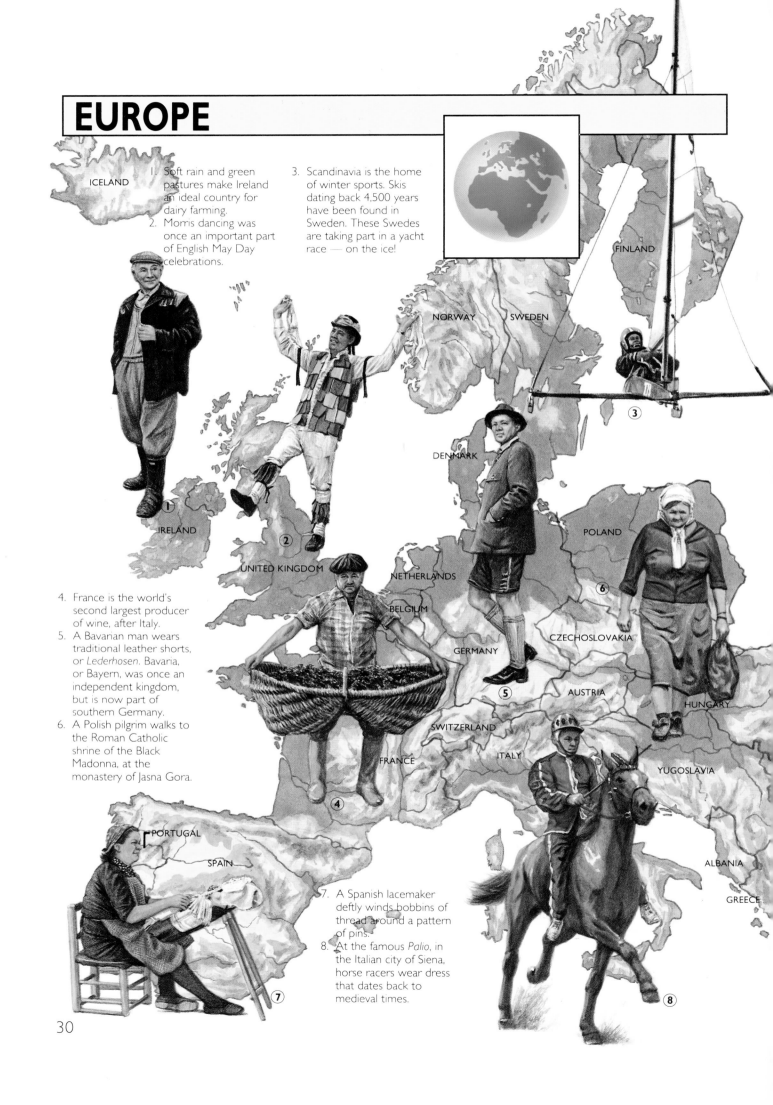

ICELAND

1. Soft rain and green pastures make Ireland an ideal country for dairy farming.
2. Morris dancing was once an important part of English May Day celebrations.
3. Scandinavia is the home of winter sports. Skis dating back 4,500 years have been found in Sweden. These Swedes are taking part in a yacht race — on the ice!

4. France is the world's second largest producer of wine, after Italy.
5. A Bavarian man wears traditional leather shorts, or *Lederhosen*. Bavaria, or *Bayern*, was once an independent kingdom, but is now part of southern Germany.
6. A Polish pilgrim walks to the Roman Catholic shrine of the Black Madonna, at the monastery of Jasna Gora.

7. A Spanish lacemaker deftly winds bobbins of thread around a pattern of pins.
8. At the famous *Palio*, in the Italian city of Siena, horse racers wear dress that dates back to medieval times.

FINLAND

NORWAY   SWEDEN

DENMARK

POLAND

NETHERLANDS

BELGIUM

GERMANY   CZECHOSLOVAKIA

AUSTRIA   HUNGARY

SWITZERLAND

FRANCE   ITALY   YUGOSLAVIA

IRELAND

UNITED KINGDOM

PORTUGAL

SPAIN

ALBANIA

GREECE

30

Parisian street
Paris is one of the most beautiful cities in Europe, famed for its art and architecture, its fashion, and its food. Nearly nine million people live in the Paris area, with about two million of these living in the city itself.

Taking a stroll in the Parisian streets one summer afternoon, you are likely to come across many traditional sights, such as street artists and flower sellers. You can also admire the characteristic *art deco* station entrances on the subway, the *Métro*.

A Slovak wedding
Dressed in traditional embroidered costume, a Slovak bride and her groom take formal leave of her parents before their wedding. Nearly five million Slovaks live in Czechoslovakia. The country is also home to Czechs, Poles, Hungarians, Gypsies, Germans, Ukrainians, and Russians.

THE continent of Europe is bordered by the Atlantic Ocean in the west, the Arctic Ocean in the north, and the Mediterranean Sea in the south. Its eastern border runs overland along the Ural Mountains of the Soviet Union. In the southeast the straits of the Bosporus, in Turkey, divide Europe from Asia.

Europe is the second smallest of all the continents, yet the power and influence of its peoples have been felt across the world. Throughout the centuries, Europeans have migrated to set up new societies, from Australia to Canada. Many European countries built up vast empires in the nineteenth century, exploiting the various resources of their colonial possessions to increase their own power and wealth. Europe itself has rich farmland and large mineral resources, which make it both an agricultural and industrial power. Its small size makes communications easy; fast freeways link the region's cities, and Europe's sea routes are the world's busiest.

31

Over the ages, Europeans and their traditions, have influenced the rest of the world in many ways. Europe has produced great thinkers, lawmakers, musicians, writers, artists, and inventors. It has also been the center of two World Wars.

Two thousand years ago, much of Europe was under the rule of the Romans. They controlled their vast Empire with a well-disciplined army, and by using their engineering skills to construct cities and roads. As the Roman Empire collapsed, Europe once again became a patchwork of small warring states. These were sometimes united by a common faith, Christianity, but were just as often divided by religious arguments.

Nation states grew up – large countries that often included within their borders peoples of various languages and cultures. Some nations went on to rule and settle other parts of the world. Today, their empires have gone, and they, too, face changes, as many people wish to see a single Europe in the future, united in peace.

East meets West

FOR 28 years, the German city of Berlin was divided in two. A concrete wall, topped with barbed wire, ran through the city center. People who tried to cross the wall without permission risked being shot.

Why was the city split?

During World War II, the German Nazi leader, Adolf Hitler, tried to conquer Europe. After his defeat, Germany was occupied by French, British, American, and Soviet troops. Berlin, the German capital, lay in the middle of the Soviet area, but was itself divided

Masks and cloaks add an air of mystery to the celebration of a festival in Venice. This beautiful Italian city was once the center of a powerful state, famed for its beautiful buildings, its wealth, and its love of pleasure. In the old days, merrymaking and masquerading took place before Lent, during which Christians fasted and prayed for 40 days.

Flamenco!

THE woman sways her body, raising her arms and swirling her skirts. She dances to the rhythm of a guitar, clapping, snapping her fingers, and shouting. She may click castanets, although these were not part of the original dance.

Flamenco is a style of music, song, and dance developed over the last 600 years in Andalusia, a region of Spain. Andalusia was ruled for centuries by Arabs. It was also the home of Gypsies – wandering people originally from India – who spread across Europe in the Middle Ages.

32

into four sectors.

Many people who lived in East Berlin disliked the Communist rule set up by the Soviets. They fled to the other occupation sectors that made up West Berlin. In 1961, the East German government built the wall to stop people leaving.

During 1989, there were many changes in Eastern Europe. On November 10, East Germans were at last allowed to visit the West freely. They swarmed over the wall and began to break it down. A new, united Europe was being born.

Sweden stretches south from the Arctic Circle. In winter, the days are very short and bitterly cold, but summer brings warmth and long, sunny days when, in the north, the sun never completely disappears below the horizon. Midsummer's Eve is celebrated with parties and fancy dress. In country villages, tall maypoles are decorated with garlands, and people dance to the music of fiddles and accordions.

The story of the people of Europe is one of many different cultures. The Hungarians and Slavic peoples such as the Poles, Czechs, Slovaks, and Russians, live on the great plains of Central and Eastern Europe. The north of the continent is home to Finns, Lapps, and people who speak Germanic languages, such as the English, Dutch, Germans, and Swedes. Celtic peoples, including the Irish, Scots, Welsh, and Bretons, live in the north-west, along the Atlantic coast. In the south, the French, Spanish, Portuguese, and Italians speak "romance" languages which have come from Latin, the language of the ancient Romans. Many peoples from Asia, Africa, and the Caribbean have settled in Europe in recent years.

The music of all these peoples came together in flamenco, which was played by the Gypsies of Andalusia.

Today, Andalusia is visited by many tourists. They love to hear flamenco and to see the colorful dancing, which is not always in strictly traditional style. However, proper flamenco can also be seen and heard, and remains very popular.

When Spanish people settled in Central and South America, they took their music with them. The influence of flamenco can be heard in the music of these countries.

England v Wales

THE crowd sings and roars as Wales clashes with England at rugby union. The game, similar to football in the U.S., was invented during a school soccer match in England, in 1823. One player broke all the rules, by picking up the ball and running with it. Today, an oval-shaped ball, like the American football, is used, and there are 15 players to a side. Rugby union is the national game of Wales, and is very popular in England and Scotland, as well as in Ireland, France, Romania, New Zealand and Australia.

Workers abroad

On trolley cars and buses in Germany and the Netherlands, it is common to hear the Turkish language being spoken. Since the 1960's, many people have come from the poorer regions of Europe to work in the richer countries. These "guest workers" have sometimes had an unfriendly reception, receiving low wages and poor housing.

33

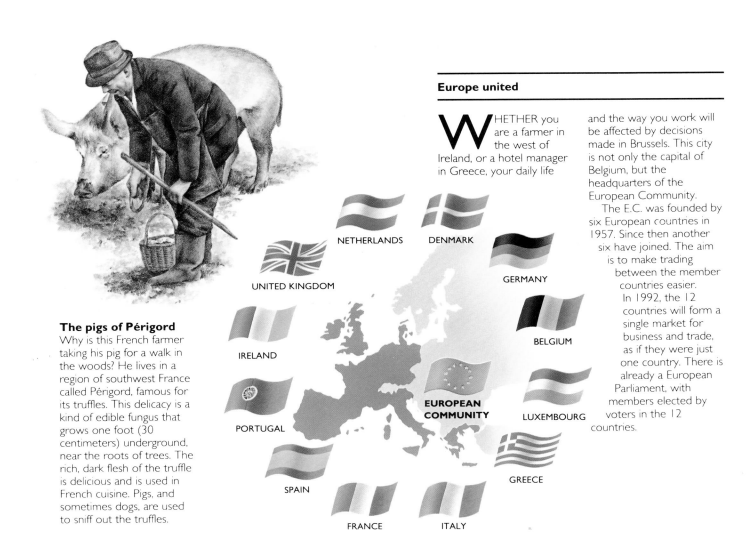

The pigs of Périgord

Why is this French farmer taking his pig for a walk in the woods? He lives in a region of southwest France called Périgord, famous for its truffles. This delicacy is a kind of edible fungus that grows one foot (30 centimeters) underground, near the roots of trees. The rich, dark flesh of the truffle is delicious and is used in French cuisine. Pigs, and sometimes dogs, are used to sniff out the truffles.

Living on a canal

Netherlands means "lowlands" and much of its land is below sea level. For hundreds of years the Dutch have been battling against water. Amsterdam is a city that was originally built on wetlands. Below the street, the old buildings are supported by long timbers, or piles. The water in the city was drained away by canals, which boats could use for transport. Today, many people still live in houseboats along the canals.

Europe united

WHETHER you are a farmer in the west of Ireland, or a hotel manager in Greece, your daily life and the way you work will be affected by decisions made in Brussels. This city is not only the capital of Belgium, but the headquarters of the European Community.

The E.C. was founded by six European countries in 1957. Since then another six have joined. The aim is to make trading between the member countries easier.

In 1992, the 12 countries will form a single market for business and trade, as if they were just one country. There is already a European Parliament, with members elected by voters in the 12 countries.

NETHERLANDS DENMARK

UNITED KINGDOM

GERMANY

IRELAND

BELGIUM

PORTUGAL

EUROPEAN COMMUNITY

LUXEMBOURG

SPAIN

GREECE

FRANCE ITALY

DID YOU KNOW?

The world's smallest country covers only 109 acres (44 hectares). It is called Vatican City, and is situated inside the Italian capital, Rome. It is the home of the Pope, head of the Roman Catholic Church. It is also the only country in the world where the official language is Latin. The Vatican city is dominated by St. Peter's Basilica (*right*), the largest church in the world.

Which country moved sideways on the map? In 1945, after World War II, Poland had to give up land on its eastern border to the Soviet Union. At the same time it was granted land in the west that was previously part of Germany.

The Icelandic parliament is the world's oldest law-making body still in existence. Called the *Althing*, it dates back to AD 930.

CLOTHES AROUND THE WORLD

IN many parts of the modern world, people dress in a similar way. Jeans and T-shirts are popular from east to west. Businessmen and women wear smart suits. Factory and farm workers wear overalls and protective clothing. However, traditional clothes are still the most practical option in some regions of the world. In very hot areas, long robes keep people cool, and headdresses or veils protect them from the sun. In the Arctic regions, wool and furs keep the Inuit, the Saami, and the Siberian hunters warm.

In many places, traditional costume is worn for special occasions or ceremonies. Costumes may be worn to show rank: for example, Western kings and queens wear crowns, and American Indian chiefs wear headdresses of eagle feathers. The way people dress often shows that they belong to a particular group. The tartan patterns of a Scottish kilt vary from one clan to another. The dress and ornaments of African herders show to which tribe, and often to which age group, they belong.

For their ceremonial dances the warriors of Papua New Guinea adorn themselves with brightly colored feathers and paint.

The colorful dress of the Peruvian Indians is woven from the wool of their alpacas, llamas, and sheep.

The *kimono* is still worn by both men and women in Japan for special occasions.

The elegant robes of this Nigerian man are woven in strips, and colored with an indigo dye.

Most Indian women continue to wear their traditional dress, the *sari*.

The Scottish kilt, a pleated skirt, is worn by both men and women.

35

Playing *pelota*
The national game of the Basque people is known as *jai alai*, or *pelota*. The ball is hurled across the court at a wall. A wickerwork scoop makes the ball travel at high speeds. The game is also popular throughout Spain, the Philippines and Latin America.

A wealth of languages

THE borders of European countries often include peoples of different origins, speaking a variety of languages. From the map, you will see that at least eight different languages are spoken in Yugoslavia. Serbo-Croat is the most widely used.

Most of the languages of Eastern Europe belong to the Indo-European group, and so are related to many of the other languages of Western Europe and Asia. However, the Hungarian language, Magyar, is not related to any of the other European languages except Finnish. They form part of the Finno-Ugric group.

	CZECH
	POLISH
	SLOVAK
	HUNGARIAN
	ROMANIAN
	SLOVENE
	SERBO-CROAT
	MONTENEGRIN
	ALBANIAN
	MACEDONIAN
	BULGARIAN
	TURKISH

POLAND

CZECHOSLOVAKIA

HUNGARY

YUGOSLAVIA

ROMANIA

BULGARIA

ALBANIA

How do the people of Europe make their living? The first Europeans were hunters and fishers. Later, they learned to farm, clearing the great forests for crops and grazing. About 250 years ago, there were great advances in science and technology. Britain became the first country in the world to build railroads, factories, and large industrial cities. The other countries of Europe soon followed, and today this industrialization has spread around the world.

Islam in Europe
About four million Muslims live in Yugoslavia, parts of which were once ruled by the Ottoman Turks. Many of the Muslims are Albanians, who live in the southern province of Kosovo. Mosques like this one are a common sight in many towns in south-eastern Europe.

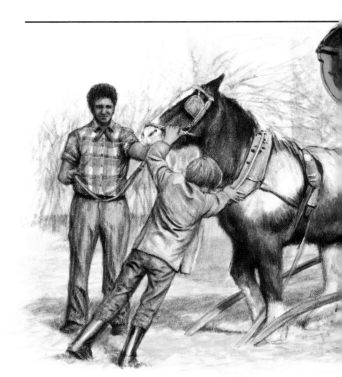

The *gorale* are farmers who live on the high slopes of Poland's Tatra Mountains. They are fiercely protective of their traditions and customs. They speak their own dialect of Polish, and wear finely embroidered costumes for special occasions, such as weddings.

As the population of Europe grew, more and more food had to be produced. However, fewer people than ever now need to work at farming and fishing. Much of their work can be carried out more easily by machines. European industry still produces cars, ships, and textiles, as well as computers and electronic goods, but faces competition from countries such as Japan and the United States. Many Europeans now work in "service" industries, such as business, international trade, or tourism. European cities such as London, Frankfurt, and Zurich are important world centers for business and finance.

Reindeer herders

THE Saami people (also called the Lapps) live on the edge of the Arctic in Norway, Sweden, Finland, and the Soviet Union. Some of the Saami continue to follow their traditional nomadic life. Every Spring they take their reindeer from the winter feeding grounds to the highland summer pastures.

On the move

THE Gypsies, or Romany people, probably originally came from India. About a thousand years ago they began to migrate west, and during the Middle Ages they spread throughout Europe. They never settled in one place, traveling instead in horse-drawn caravans, often painted in bright colors. They spoke the Romany language and lived by horse trading and metalworking. Today there are about 500,000 Gypsies left. Some have settled in towns, but others are still on the road, many in modern motor-driven caravans.

The deadly rain
Many trees and lakes in Europe have become poisoned by "acid rain." Pollution from the factory smoke and traffic fumes of the industrial cities is carried by the wind, and dropped with the rain upon the forests of Scandinavia and central Europe. Across Europe, there are campaigns for a cleaner environment.

THE SOVIET UNION

THE U.S.S.R. is a union of 15 different republics, covering over eight and a half million square miles (22 million square kilometers). It is home to 286 million people. The Russians make up half of its population, but there are over 100 other peoples living within its borders, all with their own cultures and languages. Today, many of these peoples are demanding more independence and control over their own affairs.

The way of life of the Soviet people varies greatly with the climate and landscape. The northern coast of the Soviet Union is locked in Arctic pack ice. Much of its central plains are covered in *taiga*, vast forests of pine and birch, blanketed with snow during the long winter. To the southwest lie the grasslands of the steppes, where farmers grow wheat and fruit. Deserts and mountains border the southeast.

1. This Latvian woman is performing a folk dance of her region. Latvia has been ruled by the Soviet Union since 1940, but Latvians keep their own cultural heritage alive.
2. A girl at a Moscow rock concert.

UKRAINE

③

GEORGIA

UNION OF SOVIET SOCIALIST REPUBLICS (U.S.S.R.)

KAZAKHSTAN

④

TURKMENISTAN

UZBEKISTAN

KIRGHIZIA

TADJIKISTAN

3. A man from the republic of Georgia in traditional dress of the region.

The herders of Turkmenistan
A herder of the nomadic Tekke tribe, wearing his traditional shaggy sheepskin hat. The Turkmen are famous for their beautiful carpets, which incorporate intricate, geometric designs. Many of the carpets are now woven in state-run factories in Bukhara for export.

38

The Siberian winter
Constructing an oil rig in Siberia is cold work. The average temperature in January can be as low as 59 degrees Fahrenheit (50 degrees Celsius) below zero. The Siberian region lies east of the Urals and covers over five million square miles (13 million square kilometers). It is an area rich in oil, coal, iron ore, and gold.

Hunting the seal
A Soviet Eskimo, or Yugyt, takes aim during a hunting expedition. He is wrapped in furs against the Arctic cold. A few people still manage to survive by hunting in the remote northeast. They include the Yugyt, the Chukchee, and the Koryak.

RUSSIAN SOVIET FEDERAL SOCIALIST REPUBLIC

4. An Uzbek elder in the ancient city of Samarkand. He follows the Muslim faith.
5. A Kirghiz man waits to have his fleece graded. The Kirghiz people live in felt-covered tents called *yurts*, on the high plateau near the Soviet border with China and Afghanistan.

The Mongolian border
The Buriats are one of the Mongol peoples living in the Soviet Union, Mongolia, and China. Over 300,000 Buriats live to the south of Lake Baikal, on the steppes near the Mongolian border. Many of them have given up their nomadic existence and now live in log cabins.

39

For hundreds of years the Russians were ruled by emperors, called tsars. The ordinary people were very poor and had few rights. In 1917, there was a revolution. Tsar Nicholas II was overthrown and a Communist state was established.

In 1941, the Soviet Union joined with the Allies (Britain, France, and the United States) in the war against Nazi Germany. After the end of World War II, a "cold war" was waged between the U.S. and the Soviet Union. Many people around the world feared the outbreak of war between the two superpowers. Now, as reforms take place within the Soviet Union, the cold war is over.

Women at work

A WOMAN sweeps the road while another directs the traffic. If you travel through the Soviet Union, you will see women working on the railways, driving buses, working in factories, and driving tractors in the fields. Others are doctors, engineers, teachers, and scientists. The first woman in space, Valentina Tereshkova, was a Russian. This is one result of the 1917 revolution, in which women played a leading part.

Today, 85 percent of Soviet women are employed. However, in the home little has changed. Women are still expected to do most of the cooking and housework, even after a hard day at the factory.

"Blessed is our God ...."

AMID the soaring voices of the choir, a priest raises candles as he blesses the congregation. Many Christians belong to the Russian Orthodox Church. They worship in beautiful domed churches decorated with *icons* (holy pictures).

The Orthodox faith was originally based in Constantinople, now the Turkish city of Istanbul. In AD 988 a Russian prince, Vladimir, married a sister of the Byzantine emperor and became converted to Orthodox Christianity. This became the religion of Russia's tsars. Orthodox Churches also grew up in Georgia and Armenia.

After the revolution of 1917, the Orthodox Church was no longer tolerated by the state. Two thirds of the churches were closed by the Communists. Today, people are free to follow their own beliefs, and many of the churches are being opened up once again. As well as Orthodox Christians, there are Roman Catholics, Protestants, Jews, Muslims, and Buddhists in the Soviet Union.

DID YOU KNOW?

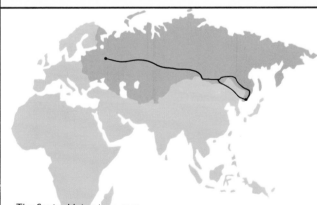

The Soviet Union is so vast that while night is falling in the west, a new day is dawning on the east coast.

The Soviet Union takes up 15 percent of the Earth's total land area.

Moscow has the busiest underground railroad system in the world. It carries up to 6,500,000 passengers a day. Its stations are elaborately decorated with marble columns, lamps, and bronze statues.

The world's longest railroad line stretches over 5,864 miles (9,438 kilometers). Passengers on the Trans-Siberian Express take over eight days to travel from Moscow to Nakhodka, on the Pacific Coast. Other long tracks branch south to China.

The coldest town in the world is Oymyakon, in Siberia, which has recorded temperatures of 76 degrees Fahrenheit (60 degrees Celsius) below zero.

On the high bar
In the Soviet Union, a talent for sport is often spotted at an early age. Children at special sports' schools receive hard training in addition to their normal lessons. Many Soviet gymnasts have won Olympic medals at an early age. Popular sports in the Soviet Union include ice hockey and ice skating.

HOUSES AROUND THE WORLD

THE first hunters took shelter in caves, or made simple huts of branches and animal hides. They needed to be able to move easily from place to place as they followed the herds of animals on which they relied for food. Some people still follow a nomadic existence today. They, too, have movable houses; the herders of North Africa and Asia live in tents made of skins, or felt; Gypsies and other travelers live in caravans.

More permanent homes are built of local wood or stone, or modern building materials such as concrete, steel, glass, and plastic. Over half the world's houses are made of mud, usually mixed with straw and water to form a sun-baked brick. Mud brick huts are ideally suited to hot climates because they are cool, and easy to build.

The location of a house may require special building methods. Houses beside rivers are often built on stilts in case of floods. Skyscrapers were first built in crowded cities, because there was no room to build outward, only upward.

The size and shape of houses may depend on the family organization. In the long houses of Southeast Asia, several families may live under one roof. In the small apartments of many Western cities, people often live on their own.

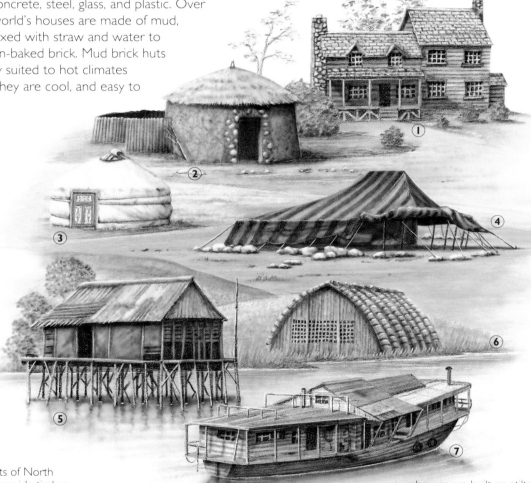

1. The forests of North America provide timber for building houses and ranches. Concrete and brick are also widely used.
2. The round, thatched hut of Central Africa is made of mud bricks, dried in the sun. Villages may be surrounded by a stockade of thorn to keep out wild animals.
3. A ger, or "yurt," is a round tent made of warm felt, and still used by the herders of Mongolia. It can withstand winds of up to 100 miles (160 kilometers) an hour.
4. The traditional tent of the Bedouin is made of goat or camel hair, stretched over a wooden frame. It offers shelter from sandstorms and heat.
5. Fish and rice farming have attracted Thai villagers to a life by the water's edge. Their houses are built on stilts.
6. The Arabs who live in the wetlands of Iraq build houses of reeds, on islands made of mud and vegetation.
7. In Hong Kong, there is little room for new buildings. Many people live on houseboats in the harbors.

ASIA

1. This Turk is preparing natural sponges for sale. They have been collected from the blue waters of the Aegean Sea.
2. This Jew lives on a *kibbutz*, a kind of communal farm, in Israel.

TURKEY

ISRAEL
JORDAN
IRAQ
KUWAIT
IRAN
SAUDI ARABIA
YEMEN
OMAN
PAKISTAN
INDIA
SRI LANKA

THE great continent of Asia is part of the same land mass as Europe. Its land border runs through Turkey and the Soviet Union. To the east it is bordered by the Pacific, and to the south by the Indian Ocean.

Western Asia is a region of deserts and mountains. Three of the great world religions, Judaism, Christianity, and Islam, were born among the people of these lands. It was here, too, that the world's first civilizations grew up, in an area between the Tigris and Euphrates rivers, called Mesopotamia. The Mesopotamians learned how to cultivate and harvest their crops. They built cities, and invented the earliest known writing, called *cuneiform* (see page 15).

3. Many women in Middle Eastern countries dress in accordance with Islamic tradition.
4. Oil is the key to wealth for the Middle Eastern countries.
5. This Indian student wears traditional jewelry and silks.
6. Knee-deep in the flooded paddy field, Vietnamese women tend the young rice plants.
7. Collecting birds' nests, the vital ingredient for birds' nest soup, a delicacy in China.
8. Balinese dancing is famous for its lavish costumes and intricate movements.

A religious life
At this temple in Thailand, young men are learning to be Buddhist monks. They have shaven heads and wear orange robes. Many of the world's religions grew up in Asia. Buddhism was founded in India by Siddhartha Gautama, who was born in about 568 BC. Over 47 million Thai people follow the Buddhist faith.

For India and freedom!
Magnificent elephants form a stately parade through Delhi, the Indian capital. Republic Day, held on January 26, marks India's independence. During the eighteenth century, European merchants siezed power in India, and, from 1858 until 1947, the country was ruled by the British.

In the south of Asia, a great triangle of land extends into the Indian Ocean. This "subcontinent" is a region of dusty plains, teeming cities, and jungles. This area, too, was the site of early civilizations, along the Indus River. Today, the Indian subcontinent is the most populous region in the world, with nearly one billion inhabitants.

Throughout its history, Southeast Asia has been invaded by outsiders – Chinese settlers, Arab traders, and Europeans in search of lands to add to their empires. In the last 40 years, countries such as Vietnam and Cambodia have been torn apart by war. There is now hope that peace will return to this beautiful region, with its green forests, rice paddies, and lush, tropical islands.

Mountain people
The Drukpa people live in Bhutan, a small kingdom high in the Himalayas. They herd yaks, shaggy-coated mountain oxen, and grow rice and barley in the valleys. They are Buddhists. Many Hindus, originally from Nepal, also live in Bhutan.

BHUTAN

BANGLADESH

MYANMAR (BURMA)

LAOS

THAILAND

CAMBODIA

VIETNAM

MALAYSIA

SINGAPORE

PHILIPPINES

INDONESIA

BALI

43

A Bedouin woman from the deserts of Saudi Arabia wears her traditional robes and veil. Most Saudi women keep their heads and faces covered in public and continue to live according to Islamic tradition. Many Bedouin still live in their black tents in the desert (see page 41), in which brightly colored "walls" woven out of goat's hair separate the men's and women's quarters.

Southwest Asia is often known as the Middle East or Near East. Closest to Europe (part of its territory lies in that continent) is Turkey. To the south are the Arab peoples of the Arabian Peninsula. Many are city dwellers but others are farmers, and the Bedouin lead a nomadic existence in the arid desert lands. Some of the Arabs of southern Iraq live in reed houses in the marshlands, fishing and breeding water buffalo.

The present day boundaries of Turkey, Syria, Iran, and Iraq divide up the traditional lands of the Kurdish peoples – nomads who lived by herding their sheep and goats. The Iranians are not Arab, but are descended from the ancient Persian peoples. To the east, Iran borders Pakistan and Afghanistan, home to the Baluchi and Pashtun peoples.

Racing camels are said to be able to keep up a speed of 12 miles (20 kilometers) per hour all day long. In Saudi Arabia special races are held for the fastest animals.

A JEWISH boy stands praying against the Western Wall in Jerusalem. This wall is holy to the Jews because it is near the site of their Temple, which was destroyed in AD 70 by the Romans. It forms part of a larger wall that surrounds the Muslim Dome of the Rock mosque. As a result it has been the subject of many battles for possession in the past.

Religious conflict is still a part of everyday life for many people in the Middle East. After World War II, when millions of Jews were persecuted and murdered by the Nazi Germans, the state of Israel was founded as a homeland for the Jewish people. This led to fighting with the Palestinian Arabs who lived in the region, and this conflict is still unresolved. In Lebanon, there is fighting between various groups of Muslims and Christians. In 1979, Shiite Muslims in Iran began an Islamic revolution, introducing strict Islamic laws. Fears about the new revolutionary government in Iran, and longstanding territorial disputes, sparked off a war between Iran and Iraq in 1980, which lasted for eight years.

A whirling dervish
At the town of Konya, in central Turkey, a man in a long robe whirls round and round in a dance. He belongs to the Mevlevi, one of various groups known as "dervishes" who dance as part of their worship. They follow the Sufi sect of Islam.

MONEY AROUND THE WORLD

TRADING has always been a point of contact between different peoples and cultures. The first traders exchanged, or "bartered," goods. Seeds were bartered for tools or woven cloth for a pig. Bartering was not an easy way to trade because it was often difficult to agree on the value of different items. All over the world, people began to use small, valuable tokens instead. All kinds of precious objects were used as money, including metal bracelets and rings, bricks of pressed tea, salt, beads, shells, and animal teeth.

The most useful tokens were metal coins. They were easy to carry, weigh, divide, or melt together. The oldest known coin was made in Lydia (now part of Turkey) over 2,500 years ago. Paper bank notes were first used in China, about 1,000 years ago.

Today, coins are used for small values of money, and bank notes for larger values. Plastic credit cards are used to transfer funds without using cash at all.

1. *Aggri* beads were once used as money in Ghana, in West Africa. They were made of colorful glass.
2. Cowrie shells were used as money on many Pacific islands, and in other parts of the world.

3. Modern bank notes are often decorated with pictures of the country or with portraits of famous people. They usually have complicated patterns on them, in order to make them difficult to copy or "forge."
4. Early coins were made of valuable metals such as gold and silver. Today's coins have little real value.
5. This ancient Chinese coin was made with a hole in the middle, so that it could be tied onto a thong.
6. On the Pacific island of Yap, in Micronesia, stones were used as money. Small stones could be bartered for goods, larger stones were often placed outside a rich person's house to display their wealth.

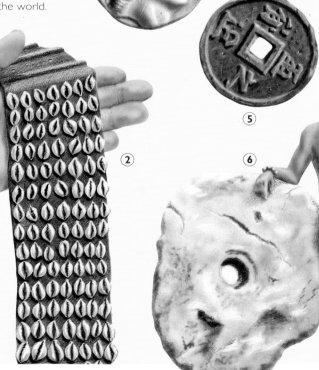

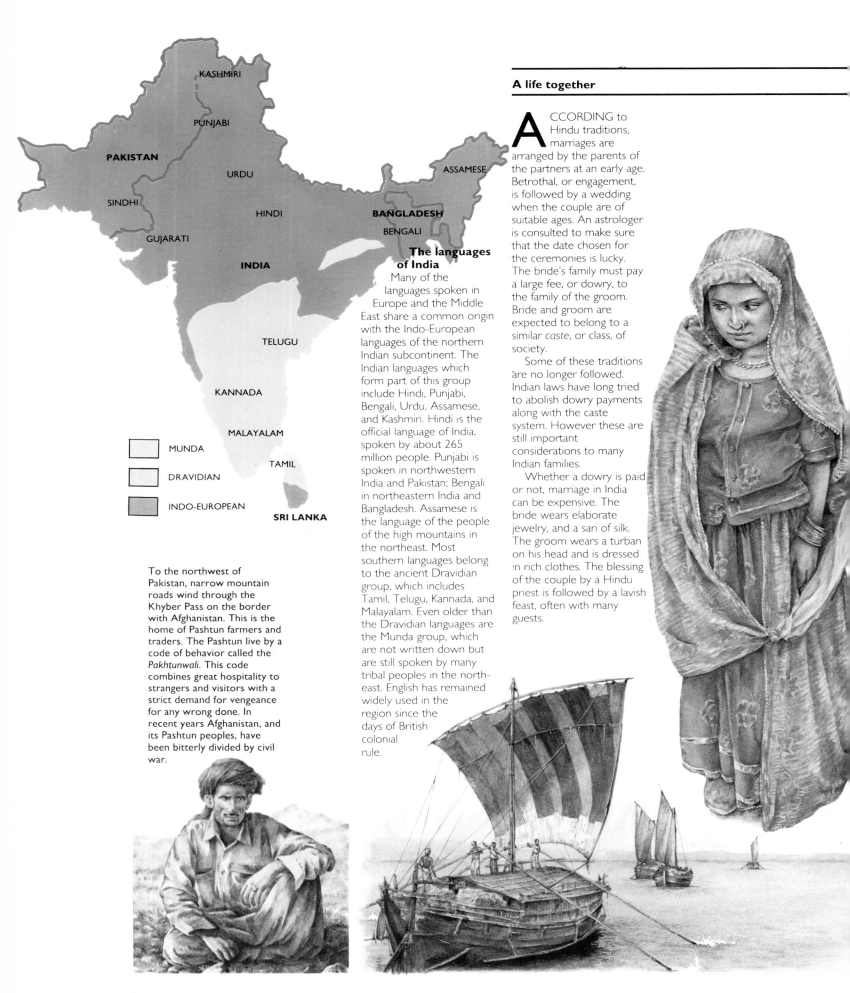

KASHMIRI

PUNJABI

PAKISTAN

URDU

ASSAMESE

SINDHI

HINDI

BANGLADESH

BENGALI

GUJARATI

INDIA

TELUGU

KANNADA

MALAYALAM

MUNDA

DRAVIDIAN

TAMIL

INDO-EUROPEAN

SRI LANKA

The languages of India

Many of the languages spoken in Europe and the Middle East share a common origin with the Indo-European languages of the northern Indian subcontinent. The Indian languages which form part of this group include Hindi, Punjabi, Bengali, Urdu, Assamese, and Kashmiri. Hindi is the official language of India, spoken by about 265 million people. Punjabi is spoken in northwestern India and Pakistan; Bengali in northeastern India and Bangladesh. Assamese is the language of the people of the high mountains in the northeast. Most southern languages belong to the ancient Dravidian group, which includes Tamil, Telugu, Kannada, and Malayalam. Even older than the Dravidian languages are the Munda group, which are not written down but are still spoken by many tribal peoples in the northeast. English has remained widely used in the region since the days of British colonial rule.

To the northwest of Pakistan, narrow mountain roads wind through the Khyber Pass on the border with Afghanistan. This is the home of Pashtun farmers and traders. The Pashtun live by a code of behavior called the *Pakhtunwali*. This code combines great hospitality to strangers and visitors with a strict demand for vengeance for any wrong done. In recent years Afghanistan, and its Pashtun peoples, have been bitterly divided by civil war.

ACCORDING to Hindu traditions, marriages are arranged by the parents of the partners at an early age. Betrothal, or engagement, is followed by a wedding when the couple are of suitable ages. An astrologer is consulted to make sure that the date chosen for the ceremonies is lucky. The bride's family must pay a large fee, or dowry, to the family of the groom. Bride and groom are expected to belong to a similar *caste*, or class, of society.

Some of these traditions are no longer followed. Indian laws have long tried to abolish dowry payments along with the caste system. However these are still important considerations to many Indian families.

Whether a dowry is paid or not, marriage in India can be expensive. The bride wears elaborate jewelry, and a sari of silk. The groom wears a turban on his head and is dressed in rich clothes. The blessing of the couple by a Hindu priest is followed by a lavish feast, often with many guests.

The great city of Bombay is the center of one of the world's most prolific movie industries. Over 800 movies are produced every year. Indian films are famous for their lavish costumes and glamorous stars. Singing and dancing are often in the traditional style.

Travelling out of Pakistan across the dusty plain of the Punjab, the Indian border is crossed near the city of Amritsar, the site of the magnificent Golden Temple which is the holiest place of the Sikh religion. Although the majority of Indians are Hindus, there are also Christians, Sikhs, Muslims, and Parsees who all follow their own religious beliefs.

India is a mixture of many different peoples. Fourteen languages are officially recognized, but many more are actually spoken. Much of Indian society is still divided by the Hindu class, or *caste*, system, although modern governments have tried to break down these divisions. The highest *caste* is that of Brahman (priest), the lowest is Sudra (artisan or laborer). Each individual is born into one caste, and traditionally cannot move, or marry, outside it.

Life on top of the world

THIS Sherpa was born and raised in sight of the world's highest mountain. Mount Everest lies on the border between Nepal and Tibet, and some tourists and climbers trek up from the Nepalese capital of Kathmandu to see the great peak for themselves.

Everest was first conquered by a Sherpa, Tenzing Norgay, together with the New Zealander, Edmund Hillary, in 1953.

Many Sherpas act as mountain guides. They are accustomed to the high altitudes, the steep rocky footpaths, and the snow. Others follow a traditional way of life, growing potatoes, radishes, barley, and buckwheat in the high valleys.

The Sherpa people follow the Buddhist faith. Nepal has many Buddhist holy sites, marked by flags and prayer wheels. These are revolving cylinders inscribed with holy texts, which are spun by pilgrims.

For followers of the Hindu faith, the Ganges is a holy river. They cleanse themselves in it at holy places, and scatter the ashes of their dead in its waters.

In Bangladesh the mouth of the Ganges divides to form a huge delta. Here, its navigable waterways carry trading vessels laden with jute and sugar cane. Floods and storms often threaten the livelihoods of the people of the delta region.

Buddhists and Hindus
A Kandyan dancer at the *Esala Perahara*, a Buddhist festival which is held every August in the town of Kandy in central Sri Lanka. Sri Lanka is the home of Sinhalese people, who are Buddhists. When Sri Lanka (then called Ceylon) was under British rule, Tamil laborers from southern India were brought over to work on the tea and coffee plantations. Sri Lanka became independent in 1948, but the years since have been marked by bitter conflict between the Buddhist Sinhalese and the Hindu Tamils.

THE western half of the island of New Guinea is ruled by Indonesia, and is called Irian Jaya. Deep in the central highlands, on the steep hillsides of the Baliem valley, lie the huts of the Dani people. The Dani still use tools of stone, wood, and bone, and light fires by rubbing sticks together. Salt is produced and has been used as a bartering commodity for centuries. Their chief crop is sweet potatoes, but pork and vegetables are eaten at special banquets to mark important festivals. Traditionally, most of the work in the fields was done by women while the men were skilled at weaving baskets and nets, braiding ropes, and making necklaces. The Dani were once a warlike people, and until recently were feared as "headhunters" and cannibals. During the last 30 years the Indonesian government has begun to develop Irian Jaya, building roads, schools, and clinics and threatening the old ways of life.

In the lands to the east of India, great rivers flow south from highland regions to the sea. Rice has been grown in the fertile valleys of these rivers for thousands of years, providing the staple diet for the peoples of the region. Many civilizations flourished here. Angkor Wat, a vast temple in the Cambodian jungle, dates from the twelfth century. Buddhism and Hinduism are the main faiths, brought to the region by Indian traders and settlers. China has also influenced this region; today, nearly 15 percent of the population of Thailand is of Chinese descent.

Riches from oil

The state of Brunei occupies two tiny portions of the island of Borneo. It became independent from British rule in 1983. It is a land of dense forest, where the people grow bananas, rice, and cassava. But nearly all of its wealth comes from oil, which is produced at the Seria oilfield and at offshore production rigs. The ruler, or Sultan, of Brunei is said to be the richest man in the world.

Javanese puppetry

Java is one of Indonesia's larger islands. It is famous for a type of rhythmic music, played by a large percussion orchestra or *gamelan*, and for its styles of dancing. Puppets are another traditional entertainment on Java. These are not the figures made of wood or plastic that are used in Western countries. Instead they are made of flat card, and moved by hand-held wires. They are operated behind a cotton screen, and lit from behind. The shadows of the puppets flicker across the screen like fantastic characters from a film. Music is played as heroes and villains do battle in well known and much loved tales.

Silver and beads

THE Akha people live in the hills of Thailand. Akha women and babies wear beautiful, elaborate head-dresses. Styles vary from region to region; the headdresses may be decorated with coins, beads, buttons, silver discs, fur, and dyed feathers. More and more items are added over the years, until a headdress can become as heavy as two pounds (four kilograms).

Thailand is an ancient kingdom which has always remained independent from European rule. It is a producer of rice, tapioca, sugar, and lumber. Tourism has become a major industry in recent years, bringing Western influences to the cities. But a traditional way of life is still followed by many of the hill peoples.

A long finger of land stretches south from Thailand towards a great chain of islands. This region is divided between Malaysia, Indonesia, the Philippines, and the small states of Singapore and Brunei. Here, too, Chinese and Indian influences have mixed with a wide variety of local cultures. The Islamic faith is widely followed, brought to the region by Arab traders, but there are also Buddhists, Hindus, and Christians.

The region was once colonized by the Dutch and the British, who grew and exported spices, rubber, and tobacco. In World War II it was invaded by the Japanese. Today, it is home to many different peoples including Malays, Dayak, Chinese, Indians, Batak, Javanese, Balinese, and Moluccans.

Beneath tall office blocks, the streets of Singapore are busy with traffic. The signs on the buildings are in Chinese, for three quarters of Singapore's population is of Chinese origin.

Singapore was set up as a British trading port in 1819 by Sir Stamford Raffles. He made it a free port, open to traders from all over the world. Many Chinese came as traders, or as laborers, locked into the holds of ships called "junks" until a prospective employer would pay for their passage.

Today, Singapore is one of the largest ports in the world, and, together with Hong Kong, the leading commercial center in Southeast Asia.

DID YOU KNOW?

The peoples of Indonesia are scattered over more than 13,000 islands. These form the world's largest island group, or archipelago. Various peoples settled on the islands, with the result that over 150 different languages and dialects have developed there over the ages.

The capital of Thailand is officially called Krungthep Mahanakhon Bovorn Ratanakosin Mahinthara-yutthaya Mahadilokpop Noparatratchathani Burirom Udomratchanivetmahasathan Amornipiman Avatarnasathit Sakkathattiyavisnukarmprasit. Most people call it Bangkok!

In some parts of Indonesia, people still live in traditional "long houses." The Sakkudei people may house up to eight families in a single building.

49

THE FAR EAST

EARLY 1,100 million people live in China — more than in any other country in the world. Every scrap of arable land must be farmed to provide enough food for so many hungry mouths. China is about the size of Europe, and within its borders there are 56 different "nationalities" or peoples. Many different languages and dialects are spoken, although standard Chinese (Mandarin) is spoken by more people than any other language on Earth.

To the north, China is bordered by the vast plains and deserts of the Mongolian People's Republic. The Korean peninsula, to the east, is divided into two countries, North and South Korea. Japan is home to a very small number of Ainu people, as well as the Japanese.

The descendants of Genghis Khan
With his bowstring taut, this Mongolian archer looks much the same as his ancestors must have. The great Mongolian warrior, Genghis Khan, conquered much of Asia and Europe during the Middle Ages. Today, archery and wrestling are skills largely reserved for sporting contests. Many Mongolians no longer live a nomadic life, but have settled in towns.

④ MONGOLIA

② ① TIBET ③

Herbs for sale
Over a million Yao people live in southern China, in the provinces of Hunan, Guangdong, and Guangxi. Yao women may still be seen wearing colorful, embroidered tunics and headdresses. This woman is selling dried herbs at a street market in Tongdao. Herbs continue to play an important part in Chinese medicine.

50

1. This Tibetan woman wears bead necklaces and braids her hair.
2. A Kazakh elder rides through Xinjiang. The Kazakhs live in China, Afghanistan, and the Soviet Union.
3. China is still being explored for oil and gas. Production rigs employ both men and women.
4. Most Mongolians belong to the Kalkha people. Some are still nomads.
5. In China, as in many parts of Asia, the peasant farmer's life is still one of back breaking toil.
6. China has the oldest civil service in the world, and there are many government officials.
7. A 16-hour day for poor wages is still common for garment makers in South Korea.
8. With bulging body, a Japanese Sumo wrestler tries to topple his opponent.

A Shinto wedding
Weddings and public festivals are celebrated with great ceremony in Japan. Dressed in traditional finery, this young Japanese bride will be married according to the rites of the Shinto religion. Shinto, the "way of the gods," is based on a respect for the spirits of nature, the family, and the state. Traditionally, the man is head of the household in Japan. He works long hours while his wife runs the home and looks after their children.

JAPAN

NORTH KOREA

SOUTH KOREA

CHINA

TAIWAN

51

Life as a Chinese student

IN 1949, China became a Communist state. School-children, students, and office workers were all expected to lend a hand with factory work and farming. During the 1980's, many reforms took place in China. Farm produce could now be sold in private markets, and foreign businesses were allowed into China. Many students wanted more freedom. During 1989, thousands of students demonstrated on Tiananmen Square in the Chinese capital, Beijing. Many were killed when soldiers opened fire on them to stop the protests.

The art of acupuncture

This dummy shows the points where needles can be inserted into the skin of the human body for the treatment known as acupuncture. This is a traditional Chinese remedy for pain and illness. The needles do not hurt the patient. Traditional Chinese medicine is very popular in China, and is now sometimes used in Western countries.

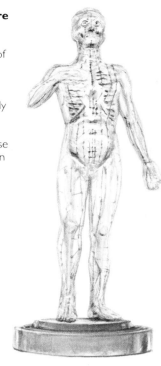

A craftworker puts the finishing touches to an enameled dish. China has a long tradition of fine craft skills. For centuries, Chinese porcelain, jade carving, and metalwork were famous around the world. Silk was first woven in China over 3,700 years ago.

The Tibetan way of life

HIGH in the pastures of the Tibetan plateau, women churn yak milk into butter. This will be mixed with tea and barley flour, or *tsampa*. The Tibetan people are Buddhists and have their own language. Many Tibetans want to be independent from China, and wish to see their religious leader, the Dalai Lama, returned from exile in India to his palace in Lhasa, the capital of Tibet.

DID YOU KNOW?

All kinds of physical exercises and martial arts are popular in China. *Tai ji quan*, known in the West as *Tai chi*, is mostly made up of slow, graceful body movements. At dawn, many people can be seen in city parks practicing these movements.

Before the Communists came to power in China, it was common practice to bind up the feet of some young girls. The small size of their deformed feet was thought to be a sign of beauty. Today, such cruel practices are banned, but old women may still be seen hobbling along.

The soybean story

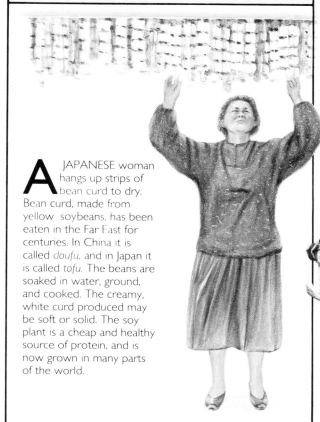

A JAPANESE woman hangs up strips of bean curd to dry. Bean curd, made from yellow soybeans, has been eaten in the Far East for centuries. In China it is called *doufu*, and in Japan it is called *tofu*. The beans are soaked in water, ground, and cooked. The creamy, white curd produced may be soft or solid. The soy plant is a cheap and healthy source of protein, and is now grown in many parts of the world.

Rice farming in Japan

RICE is eaten with almost every meal in Japan. It is grown in lush paddy fields watered by heavy seasonal rains. In the last 30 years, the number of Japanese who live by farming has fallen, as machines do much of the time-consuming heavy labor. This machine plants rice automatically. Others are used to plough the paddy fields, thresh and dry the grain. Japan produces all the rice it needs, despite the fact that much of the land is mountainous, and unsuitable for farming.

A Japanese businessman takes part in the tea ceremony. This ancient Japanese ritual has become a formal celebration of courtesy and order over the centuries. It is still widely practiced in Japan.

Remembering the past

From 1392 until 1910, Korea was ruled by the Yi dynasty. In 1910, it became part of the Japanese Empire. After World War II it was divided into communist North Korea, and capitalist South Korea. Here, a descendant of the Yi royal family honors his ancestors at the Chongmyo shrine in Seoul, the capital of South Korea. The honoring of one's ancestors developed from the ideas of the Chinese philosopher Kong Fuzi, known to the Western world as Confucius. He believed in social order, and respect for one's elders and rulers.

Festival time

IT IS November 15, and this Japanese boy is wearing traditional dress for his 7-5-3 celebration. On this date, boys aged five and girls aged three and seven visit religious shrines to ensure a happy and prosperous future. Other children's festivals include Girls' Day on March 3, and Boys' Day on May 5. The whole family joins in these celebrations, as well as those at New Year, and at the Midsummer O-Bon Festivals.

53

OCEANIA

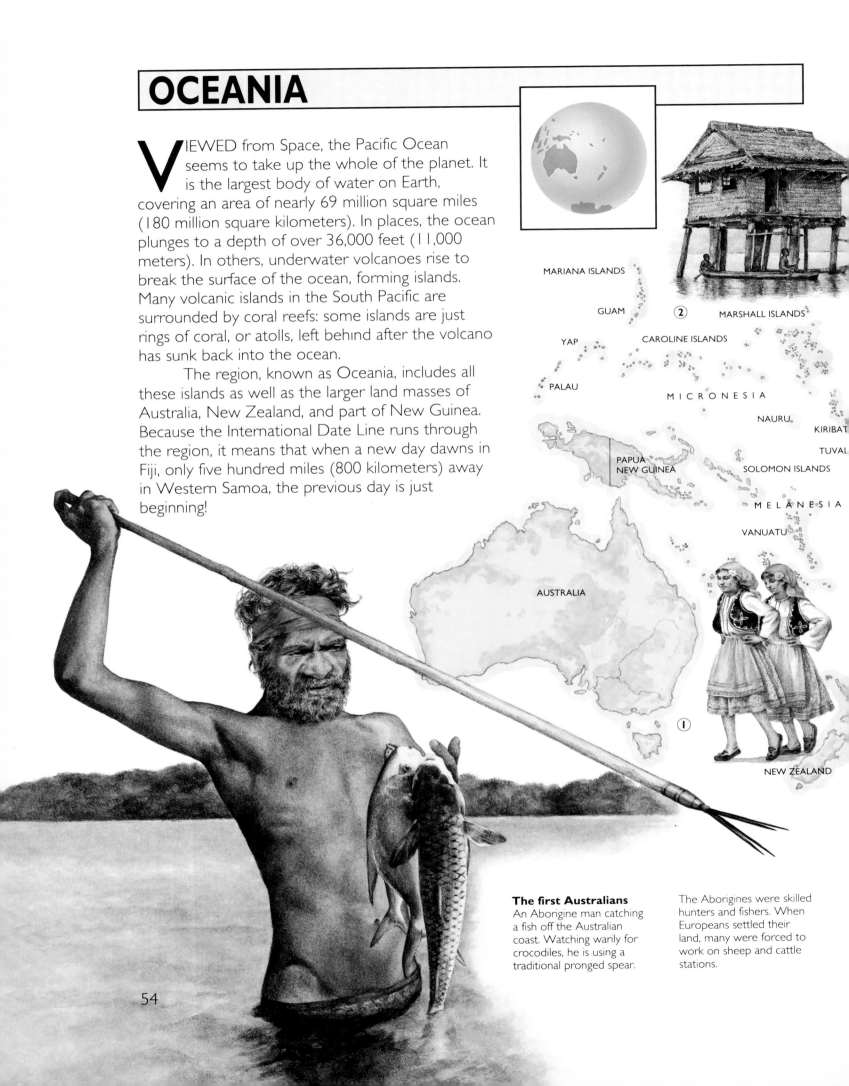

VIEWED from Space, the Pacific Ocean seems to take up the whole of the planet. It is the largest body of water on Earth, covering an area of nearly 69 million square miles (180 million square kilometers). In places, the ocean plunges to a depth of over 36,000 feet (11,000 meters). In others, underwater volcanoes rise to break the surface of the ocean, forming islands. Many volcanic islands in the South Pacific are surrounded by coral reefs: some islands are just rings of coral, or atolls, left behind after the volcano has sunk back into the ocean.

The region, known as Oceania, includes all these islands as well as the larger land masses of Australia, New Zealand, and part of New Guinea. Because the International Date Line runs through the region, it means that when a new day dawns in Fiji, only five hundred miles (800 kilometers) away in Western Samoa, the previous day is just beginning!

MARIANA ISLANDS

GUAM ② MARSHALL ISLANDS

YAP CAROLINE ISLANDS

PALAU

M I C R O N E S I A

NAURU

KIRIBAT

TUVAL

PAPUA
NEW GUINEA SOLOMON ISLANDS

M E L A N E S I A

VANUATU

AUSTRALIA

①

NEW ZEALAND

The first Australians
An Aborigine man catching a fish off the Australian coast. Watching warily for crocodiles, he is using a traditional pronged spear.

The Aborigines were skilled hunters and fishers. When Europeans settled their land, many were forced to work on sheep and cattle stations.

54

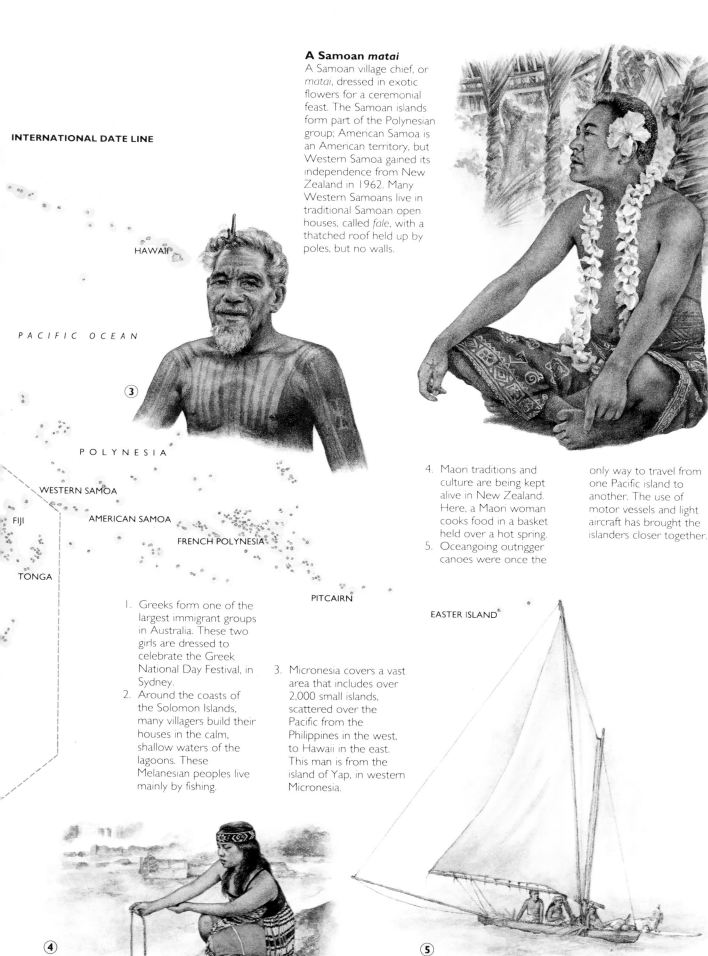

INTERNATIONAL DATE LINE

HAWAII

PACIFIC OCEAN

③

POLYNESIA

WESTERN SAMOA

FIJI

AMERICAN SAMOA

FRENCH POLYNESIA

TONGA

PITCAIRN

EASTER ISLAND

A Samoan *matai*

A Samoan village chief, or *matai*, dressed in exotic flowers for a ceremonial feast. The Samoan islands form part of the Polynesian group; American Samoa is an American territory, but Western Samoa gained its independence from New Zealand in 1962. Many Western Samoans live in traditional Samoan open houses, called *fale*, with a thatched roof held up by poles, but no walls.

4. Maori traditions and culture are being kept alive in New Zealand. Here, a Maori woman cooks food in a basket held over a hot spring.
5. Oceangoing outrigger canoes were once the only way to travel from one Pacific island to another. The use of motor vessels and light aircraft has brought the islanders closer together.

1. Greeks form one of the largest immigrant groups in Australia. These two girls are dressed to celebrate the Greek National Day Festival, in Sydney.
2. Around the coasts of the Solomon Islands, many villagers build their houses in the calm, shallow waters of the lagoons. These Melanesian peoples live mainly by fishing.

3. Micronesia covers a vast area that includes over 2,000 small islands, scattered over the Pacific from the Philippines in the west, to Hawaii in the east. This man is from the island of Yap, in western Micronesia.

④

⑤

55

Australian sheep farms, or stations, often cover huge areas of land. The sheep are rounded up using horses, jeeps, motorbikes, and even helicopters. Life in the outback can be tough. The land is hot and dusty, and the nearest neighbors are often hundreds of miles away.

Australia is the sixth largest country in the world, but only 16 million people live there. That is less than one tenth of the population of the United States. Much of the land is "outback" — dry bush country or desert, where it is hard to make a living. However, there are also areas of lush rain forest, mountains, and pasture. It is said that there are ten sheep for every human in Australia.

The first Australian peoples arrived from Southeast Asia about 40,000 years ago. They lived by hunting, and gathering nuts, plants, and fruits. Their way of life was not disturbed until the arrival of the first European settlers in 1788.

Dreamtime dancers
With his body painted and adorned with leaves, these Gagudju Aborigines dance at an Aboriginal gathering, called a *corroboree*. They perform to the sound of the didgeridoo — a hollowed out tree trunk which produces a deep, droning sound when the player blows into it. Some of the dances reenact tribal battles, some are based on animal movements such as the kangaroo dance.

The Aborigines of Australia used tools and weapons of wood and stone, including the famous boomerang. They believed that their

The peopling of a continent

IN 1788, the British founded a colony for convicts on the site of Sydney. This marked the beginning of the settlement of Australia by people from the other side of the world. However, the land was already the home of Aborigines, who had lived there for many thousands of years. When the Europeans arrived, there were about 300,000 Aborigines living in Australia. Soon they were far outnumbered by newcomers. The settlers had a very different way of life, and they changed the face of the continent as they farmed the land, and mined for gold and other minerals such as tin, copper, nickel, and zinc.

People are still arriving in Australia today, from Britain, Ireland, Scandinavia, the Netherlands, Italy, Greece, and many Asian countries. From this mixture of cultures a new nation is being created.

1901
BRITISH AND IRISH
OTHER EUROPEANS
ASIAN
NEW ZEALANDERS
AMERICAN
AFRICAN
OTHERS

The two charts show the number of people living in Australia, but born in a foreign country in 1901, and 1986.

land was created by spirits long ago, in the "dreamtime."

When the Europeans arrived, they stole the Aborigines' land. Many Aborigines were killed, or died of new, imported diseases. Their population dwindled from about 300,000 at the time of the arrival of the first European settlers, to about 60,000 by the 1900's. Today, however, many Aborigines are interested once again in their ancient culture. They are demanding rights over their tribal lands, better housing, and jobs. Some Aborigines have settled in tribal communities, on territory set aside by the government. Although they can no longer live a nomadic existence, they are free to hunt and preserve their culture through paintings, dance, and song.

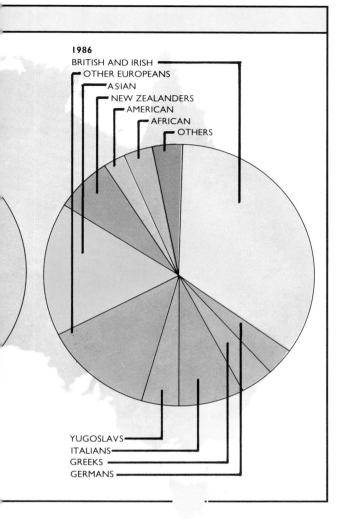

1986
BRITISH AND IRISH
OTHER EUROPEANS
ASIAN
NEW ZEALANDERS
AMERICAN
AFRICAN
OTHERS

YUGOSLAVS
ITALIANS
GREEKS
GERMANS

One thousand two hundred miles (2,000 kilometers) across the Tasman Strait lies New Zealand, a nation made up of two main islands and many smaller ones. To the east it faces the great expanse of the South Pacific. New Zealand has a cool, mild climate and is home to many plants and birds seen nowhere else on Earth, such as the kakapo and the kiwi.

New Zealand is sheep farming country and is also famed for its dairy produce. However of the three and a half million people, only ten percent work on the land. Most live in cities such as Auckland, Wellington, and Christchurch, working in industry or business.

The Maori people

ABOUT 295,000 Maoris live in New Zealand, descendants of Polynesian settlers who sailed west across the Pacific over a thousand years ago. The Maoris fought the European settlers, who arrived in the nineteenth century in an attempt to hold on to their traditional lands. Today, many New Zealanders are working to keep Maori culture alive. These youngsters are performing a traditional dance, with stamping, chanting, and singing, at a Maori festival.

A Pacific nation
New Zealand governs various Pacific islands, and numbers of Samoans and Cook Islanders live in New Zealand. The Maoris themselves are a Polynesian people. Most New Zealanders are of European descent, and English is the common language.

Australian lifesavers strain at the oars in a surfboat race at a surf lifesaver's carnival. The Australian sunshine attracts surfers, swimmers, and sunbathers to the beautiful beaches. Bands of volunteer lifeguards patrol the beaches, ready to help surfers or swimmers in distress. During the southern summer, life can be spent outdoors, with beach parties, sailing, and sports.

A boar's head mask from Melanesia. Many of the old religious beliefs of the Pacific have been replaced by Christianity. Often, though, the people of the islands have mixed Christianity with the spirits, ghosts, sorcery, and magic which made up their traditional beliefs.

The gift of a pig

A PIG means wealth to the Kawelka people of Papua New Guinea. It is not only cooked at feasts, but exchanged instead of money when a man pays for his bride. People who own many pigs are thought to be important members of society. If they are generous and give many pigs away, they will be treated as leaders. At a ceremony called a *moka*, gifts are given to important people.

Heads of stone

The soil on Easter Island, in the eastern Pacific, is dug away to reveal colossal figures of stone. There are over 600 of these huge statues on the island. They were carved and erected by Polynesians some time between the years AD 1000 and 1600, although exactly how and when is one of the world's great mysteries.

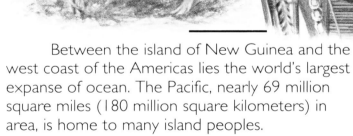

Between the island of New Guinea and the west coast of the Americas lies the world's largest expanse of ocean. The Pacific, nearly 69 million square miles (180 million square kilometers) in area, is home to many island peoples.

The island chains of Melanesia include Papua New Guinea, Fiji, New Caledonia, Vanuatu, and the Solomon Islands. Melanesian peoples are mostly black-skinned, with curly hair. Their islands were colonized by Britain and France during the nineteenth century, and in places settled by Indians and other Asian peoples. Most of the islands are now independent. For centuries the only transport between the thousands of Melanesian islands was by canoe. As a result of this isolation, hundreds of different languages and cultures developed.

Shell money

The root of the *taro*, or *ndalo*, plant is poisonous — until it is boiled. It is then used as a basic ingredient for cooking on islands such as Fiji. Sometimes a great feast is held. Food might include cassava, yam, chicken, fish, pork, vegetables, coconut, pineapple, and banana.

About 700 different languages are spoken in Papua New Guinea alone.

Fiji is made up of about 320 small islands in addition to its chief centers of Vanua Levu and Viti Levu.

Today, light aircraft and fast boats link the islands of the Pacific. North of Melanesia lie the islands which make up the region known as Micronesia. Most of the islands are small coral islands. The largest island in the region is Guam, and even this is only 212 square miles (550 square kilometers) in area. The Micronesians are skilled seafarers.

The Polynesian group stretches from New Zealand in the south to Hawaii in the north, and Easter Island in the east. This region includes high volcanic islands and low atolls, coral islands which ring peaceful lagoons.

Women from the Southern Highlands of Papua New Guinea on their way home from market. They carry their purchases in *bilums*, brightly colored string bags which are used throughout Papua New Guinea.

A Tongan war dance
The Pacific islanders are famous for their beautiful dancing, performed at feasts and on public occasions. This dance was once part of preparations for war. However, the islands of Tonga have enjoyed peace for over a hundred years.

Fire walkers of Fiji

THESE Indians from Mbengga in Fiji are performing a fire walking ritual at a Hindu temple, as part of a religious festival. Boulders in a pit are heated with burning logs. Then, walkers step through the pit, without appearing to feel any pain,
or injuring themselves.

Many Indians were brought to Fiji by the British, when the islands were under colonial rule, to work on the sugar plantations. In time there were more Indians living on
the island than Fijians. This has been the source of much conflict since 1970, when Fiji gained independence.

THE Lau people live on islands they have built themselves. Their huts are constructed on rocks piled up in the shallow lagoon waters of Malaita Island, in the Solomon Islands. When it is time for a wedding, a Lau bride decorates herself with ropes of shells. Traditionally, shells, or the teeth of porpoises and bats, have been used in the Pacific instead of money. The shells used at a wedding represent the dowry, or bridal price.

GLOSSARY

Aborigine 1. The earliest known inhabitants of any country.
2. A descendant of the first Australian peoples who migrated to Australia about 40,000 years ago.

Arab A people originating in Arabia. Modern day Arabs inhabit an area from Morocco in the west to Iraq in the east. Arabs speak the Arabic language and follow the Islamic faith. Their language shows them to be one of the Semitic peoples, related to the Jews.

Bantu A group of peoples speaking related languages, who live in central and southern Africa. The group includes the Zulu, Shona, Sotho, Swazi, Ndebele, and Xhosa.

Barter A system of trade in which goods are exchanged, or swapped.

Berber A group of peoples living in the mountains and deserts of North Africa who share a common language.

Buddhism A set of beliefs based on the teachings of Siddhartha Gautama (Buddha) (c.563-c.483 BC). Buddhists believe that selflessness can lead to freedom from suffering. Various sects are based in Tibet, Sri Lanka, Southeast Asia, and Japan.

Capitalism An economic system based upon private ownership. People who operate in a capitalist society are free to manage their businesses or property for profit in competitive conditions.

Christianity A belief that Jesus Christ (?c.6 BC-c.AD 29) was the Son of God. The Christian Bible is made up of the Old Testament, which is also honored by Jews and Muslims, and by the New Testament, which tells of the teachings of Jesus. The chief sects are Protestants, Roman Catholics, and followers of the Orthodox Church.

Civilization An organized society which has made advances in the arts and sciences. For example, the ancient Mayan civilization of Central America built complex cities and temples.

Cold War A long period of hostility in which war does not break out. From the 1950's until the 1980's the United States and the Soviet Union were enemies, but did not officially fight each other.

Colony 1. A country ruled by another. Much of Africa was ruled by Britain and France during the colonial period in the nineteenth and twentieth centuries.
2. A settlement of people in a foreign land.

Communism A system of social organization in which private ownership is replaced by state ownership and management of factories and land.

Continent A large, continuous mass of land, such as Africa.

Culture 1. The customs and way of life of a group of people.
2. The world of ideas, arts, and sciences within a civilization.

Currency The system of money used in a country.

Descendants People who share a common ancestry.

Dialect Any regional, non standard variant of a language.

Dravidian A group of peoples speaking related languages and living in southern and central India. They include the Tamils, and number over 150 million.

Empire 1. A region ruled by an emperor.
2. A number of conquered lands joined under a single ruler.

Famine A life-threatening shortage of food, often caused by drought and crop failures.

Hindu A follower of Hinduism, one of the religions of India. Hinduism is based on ancient teachings set down in the Vedas or, scriptures. Hindus believe in the three gods Brahma, Shiva, and Vishnu from whom all other gods and goddesses spring. All living creatures have souls, and make progress through many lives, or "incarnations."

Immigrant Somebody who goes to live in another country or region.

Independent A country free from foreign rule.

Indian 1. An inhabitant of India.
2. A native American. When the European explorer Christopher Columbus reached the Americas, he thought he had sailed to India by a westward route. Mistakenly, he called the inhabitants "Indians."

Inhabitant A person who lives in a particular town or region.

Inuit The first European settlers in North America borrowed an Indian word to describe the people of the Arctic: *Eskimos* or *Esquimaux* meant "eaters of raw meat." The Eskimos called themselves *Inuit*, which means "the People." The word Inuit is now generally used instead of Eskimo.

Irrigation The watering of dry land so that crops can be grown. Water is carried or pumped to the fields through pipes or channels.

Islam The belief that there is one God, Allah, and that his greatest prophet was Muhammad (AD 570-632). Muhammad's beliefs are expressed in the Koran, the holy book of Islam. The prophets of the Bible are also honored. Sects include the Sunni and the Shiite Muslims.

Jew
1. One of a people originating in the deserts of the Middle East, related to the Arabs. Scattered through the world after the Romans sacked Jerusalem in AD 70, many Jews returned to the Middle East in the twentieth century. They founded the state of Israel in 1948.
2. A follower of Judaism.

Judaism The religion of the Jews. Its laws were set down 3,000 years ago in the books of Moses, which form the basis of the Hebrew scripture, or Torah, as well as the Old Testament of the Bible. Jews believe in one God, Yahweh or Jehovah.

Land mass A great body of land. Asia and Europe form a single land mass.

Latin America Mexico, Central, and South America — a region where Spanish or Portuguese is the chief language.

Maori A native New Zealander, one of a Polynesian people.

Mestizo A person of mixed Spanish and American Indian descent.

Migrant worker Somebody who travels from one place to another in search of work.

Migrate To travel a long distance.

Mormon A follower of the Church of Jesus Christ of Latter-Day Saints, a sect founded in the United States in 1830 by Joseph Smith.

Muslim A follower of Islam.

Native Born in, or originating from, a region or area.

"New World" The name given to North and South America by the first European settlers.

Nomad Someone who does not settle in one place, but moves in search of hunting, pasture lands, or trade.

"Old World" The part of the world that was known before the European discovery of the Americas: Europe, western Asia, and North Africa.

Population The number of people living within any given area.

Race Within a single species, a group of living creatures sharing the same appearance or genetic characteristics. Human beings all belong to the same species, which scientists call *Homo sapiens*.

Religion Belief or faith in a god or gods, and the system of worship that is followed.

Republic An independent democratic nation whose head of state is elected by the people. France is a republic, but Britain is a democratic monarchy, headed by a king or queen, but with democratically elected leaders.

San A desert people of southern Africa, sometimes known as Bushmen. They are skilled hunters of slight build with light brown skins.

Sect A group of people within a religious tradition who share the same beliefs or rituals.

Shanty town A poor city suburb, roughly built of shacks and sheds.

Sikh A follower of the faith founded in India by Guru Nanak Singh in about AD 1500. Male Sikhs wear beards and their long hair is tied up under a turban.

Slave A person who is treated as the property of another. Slaves are forced to work for no pay.

Slum A rundown area of a town, with poor housing conditions.

Staple food The basic part of a diet, such as rice or bread.

Subcontinent A large mass of land which forms a distinct part of a continent. The Indian subcontinent is part of Asia.

Suburbs The outlying districts of a city.

Tribe A group of people of common descent, with their own customs and traditions. The Iceni were an ancient Celtic tribe who lived in what is now East Anglia, in England.

INDEX

A

Aborigines, Australian 7, 9, 54, 56
Afar people 28
Afghanistanis 44, 46, 51
Africans 7, 8, 18, 22-9, 33, 35, 41, 56, 57
Ainu people 50
Akha people 48-9
Albanians 36
Amazon, R. 16, 17, 20
Americas, peoples of the 10-14, 16-21, 26, 27, 33, 36, 41, 56, 57
Amharic language 29
Amish sect 14
Amritsar 47
Amsterdam 34
Andalusia 32-3
Andes Mts. 16, 17, 20
Angkor Wat 48
Angola 29
Arabs 7, 9, 23, 24, 25, 32, 41, 43, 44, 49
    Arabic language 15, 29
Arawak people 18
Arctic, peoples of the 10, 14, 35, 37
Argentinians 16, 20, 21
Armenia 40
Asians 7, 9, 15, 27, 33, 41, 42-4, 46, 53, 56, 57, 58
Assamese language 46
Atlas Mts. 22, 24
Australians 7, 9, 33, 54-6, 57
Aymara Indians 17
Aztec people 19

B

Balinese people 42, 49
Baluchi people 44
Bangkok 49
Bangladesh 6, 46, 47
Bantu languages 8, 29
Basque people 36

Batak people 49
Bavarians 30
Bedouin people 41, 44
Beijing (Peking) 52
Belgium 34
Bengali language 46
Berber peoples 7, 22
    language 29
Berlin 32-3
Bhutan 43
Bolivians 17, 20, 21
Bombay 47
Botswana 29
Brazilians 16, 17, 20
Bretons 33
British people 18, 29, 30, 33, 35, 36, 43, 48, 49, 56, 57, 58, 59
Brunei 48
Brussels 34
Buddhism 40, 42, 47, 48, 49, 52
Buenos Aires 16
Bukhara 38
Bulgarians 15
Buriat people 39
Burundi 28
Bushmen see San people

C

Cambodians 43, 48
Canadians 10, 12, 14
Caribbean peoples 16, 17, 18, 33
Celtic peoples 33
Chicago 13, 14
Chileans 20, 21
Chinese peoples 9, 13, 27, 42, 43, 45, 48, 49, 50-2
    language 15, 20
Christianity 24, 30, 32, 34, 40, 42, 44, 47, 49, 58
Coptic church 24
Costa Ricans 19
Cubans 18
Czechs 31, 33

D

Dani people 48
Dayaks 49
Delhi 43
'dervishes' 44
Dinka people 24, 25, 28, 29
Dravidians see Tamils
Drukpa people 43
Dutch people 18, 29, 34, 49
    language 20, 33

E

Easter I. 58
Ecuador 16, 20
Egyptians 22, 24
    Ancient 15, 23, 25
English language 15, 20, 33, 46, 57
Eskimos see Inuit people
Ethiopians 23, 24, 29
Euphrates, R. 8, 42
Europeans 7, 9, 23, 30-4, 36-8, 43, 54, 56-7

F

Fijians 58-9
Finns 33, 36, 37
French people 18, 20, 25, 27, 30, 33, 34, 58
    language 15
Fulani people 22, 26

G

Ganges, R. 47
Georgians (Soviet Union) 38, 40
Germans 29, 30, 31-2, 34, 40, 44, 57
    Germanic languages 15, 33
Ghanaians 27, 45

Great Rift Valley 28
Greeks 55, 57
Greenland 6, 10
Guam 59
Guatemalans 16, 19
Gypsies 31, 32-3, 37, 41

H

Haitians 20
Hausa people 26
Hindi language 15, 20, 46
Hindus 43, 46, 47, 48, 49, 59
Holland see Dutch people
Hong Kong 6
Hottentots see Khoi people
Hungarians 31, 33, 36
Huns 9

I

Iceland 34
Inca people 16, 20, 21
India, peoples of 7, 27, 35, 43,
  46, 49, 58, 59
Indians, North American 6, 8,
  11, 12, 35
Indo-European languages 36, 46
Indonesia 48, 49
Inuit people 6, 10, 14, 35
Iranians 44
Iraqis 41, 44
Irian Jaya 48
Irish people 30, 33, 56, 57
Islam 9, 24, 36, 40, 42, 44, 47,
  49
Israelis 42, 44
Italians 25, 30, 32, 33, 57

J

Japanese peoples 27, 35, 50, 51,
  53
  language 15
Java 9, 20, 49
Jerusalem 44
Jewish people 10, 40, 42, 44

K

Kalahari Desert 29
Kalkha people 51
Kamba people 22
Kashmiri language 46
Kawelka people 58
Kayapo Indians 20
Kazakhs 51
Kenyans 22, 26, 28
Khoi people 7
Kinshasa 26
Kirghiz people 39
Koreans 50, 53
Kurdish people 44

L

La Paz 21
Lagos (Nigeria) 26
Lapps see Saami people
Latin language 17, 33
Latvians 38
Lau people 58
Lebanon 44
Leeward Is. 18
Lingalla language 26
Luo language 29

M

Magyar language 36
Malaysia 49
Mali 26
Maoris 7, 55, 57
Masai people 28, 29
Mayans 16, 19
Mbuti pygmies 22, 26, 28
Melanesians 55, 58
Mennonites 14
Mesopotamians 8, 42
Mexican peoples 16, 17, 19, 27
Micronesians 55, 59
Moluccan people 49
Mongolians 39, 41, 50, 51
Mormon faith 12
Moscow 38, 40
Munda languages 46
Muslims see Islam

N

Namibia 29
Navajo Indians 12
Ndebele people 22, 29
Nepal 47
Netherlands see Dutch people
New Guinea see Papua New
  Guinea
New York 10, 13
New Zealanders 33, 47, 54, 55,
  56, 57
Newfoundlanders 14
Niger 23
Nigerians 22, 23, 24, 25, 26, 35
Nile, R. 8, 24-5, 29
Nok civilization 23
Norway 37
Nuba people 25
Nubian peoples 25
Nuer people 24, 25, 29

O

Oceania 7, 9, 54-9
Orthodox Christians 40

P

Pacific Ocean 7, 9, 54-9
Pakistanis 44, 46
Palestinian Arabs 44
Papua New Guinea 35, 48, 54,
  58-9
Paris 31
Parsees 47
Pashtun people 44, 46
Patagonia 21
Périgord 34
Persians 44
Peruvians 17, 20, 21, 35
Philippinos 36, 49
Phoenicians 25
Pilgrim Fathers 12
Poles 30, 31, 33, 34, 37
Polynesians 7, 8, 9, 55, 57-9
Portuguese people 17, 29
  language 15, 20, 33
Punjab 46, 47
Pygmy peoples 22, 26, 28

Q

Québec province 10
Quechua Indians 16
Quiché Indians 19
Quito 16

R

Rastafarian faith 18
Rio de Janeiro 17, 20
Roman Catholicism 30, 34, 40
Romanians 33
Romans 25, 32, 33, 44
Romany people see Gypsies
Russians 31, 33, 38, 40
  language 15
Rwanda 28

S

Saami people (Lapps) 33, 35, 37
Sahara 23, 24, 25
Sahel 23, 26
Sakkudei people 49
Salt Lake City 12
Samarkand 39
Samoans 55
San Francisco 13
San people 7, 29
Saudi Arabians 44
Scots 33, 35
Seoul 53
Serbo-Croat language 15, 36
Sherpa people 47
Shilluk people 22, 25, 29
Shinto religion 51
Shona language 29
Siberians 35, 39, 40
Siena 30
Sikhs 47
Singapore 49
Sinhalese people 47
Slavic peoples 33
Slovaks 31, 33
Solomon Is. 55, 58
South Africans 22, 28, 29
Soviet Union 31, 32-3, 34, 37,
  38-40, 51

Spaniards 16, 17, 18, 21, 25, 30,
  32-3, 36
  language 15, 20
Sri Lankans 47
Sudanese peoples 22, 24, 25
Sumerians 15
Suriname 20
Swahili language 29
Swedes 30, 33, 37
Sydney 55, 56

T

Tamils 7, 47
  Dravidian languages 46
Tanala people 18
Tanzanians 22, 28
Tatra Mts. 37
Texans 10
Thai people 41, 42, 48, 49
Tibetans 47, 51, 52
Tigris, R. 8, 42
Titicaca, L. 17
Tongans 59
Tuareg people 24, 25
Turkmen people 38
Turks 31, 33, 36, 42, 44, 45
Tutsi people 28
Tzotzil Indians 16

U

Ugandans 28
Ukrainians 31
United States of America 11-14,
  40
Ural Mts. 31, 39
Urdu language 46
Uzbeks 39

V

Vatican City 34
Venice 32
Vietnamese people 42, 43
Vikings 9, 11

W

Washington D.C. 11
Welsh people 21, 33

X

Xhosa people 28, 29

Y

Yao people 50
Yoruba people 22, 26
Yugoslavians 36, 57
Yugyts 39

Z

Zaïrean peoples 22, 26, 28
Zanzibar 22
Zimbabweans 22
Zulus 29